THE CLIMBER'S BIBLE

The nose of El Capitan, Yosemite, California. (*R. Shaw*)

THE CLIMBER'S BIBLE

A Complete Basic Guide
to Rock and Ice Climbing and
an Introduction to Mountaineering

ROBIN SHAW

DOUBLEDAY & COMPANY, INC., GARDEN CITY, NEW YORK
1983

Also by Robin Shaw:

Running
Batik: A New Look at an Ancient Art

Library of Congress Cataloging in Publication Data

Shaw, Robin.
   The climber's bible.

   Includes bibliographies.
   1. Rock climbing.   2. Snow and ice climbing.
3. Mountaineering.   4. Mountaineering—France.
5. Mountaineering—Scotland.   6. Mountaineering—
California.   I. Title.
GV200.2.S47   1983   796.5'223
ISBN: 0-385-14075-4
Library of Congress Catalog Card Number 78–20097

9 8 7 6 5 4 3 2

Climb the mountains and get their good tidings. Nature's peace will flow into you as sunshine flows into trees. The winds will blow their own freshness into you, and the storms their energy, while cares will drop off like autumn leaves.

— JOHN MUIR

For Andy, Jimmy, George, Ian, Jennifer, Roger, Dougal, Robin, Paul, Malcolm, Morton, David, Bob, Stan, Philip, Barbara, Will, Tony, and all the many others who have made it possible

CONTENTS

INTRODUCTION

It was my first climb. The day was perfect and above me the steep slope of the mountain seemed to stretch forever, the white snow vivid against the blue sky. I was apprehensive, and as we made our way upward over easy angled ground, I thought of—and dismissed—a variety of excuses that would let me return to the horizontal world.

Still, despite my fear, I was exhilarated and had every confidence in my companion, Andy. In my gloved hand I clumsily held the ice axe that he had borrowed for me. Though I was not sure quite what to do with it, it gave me a feeling of power, as did the old hemp rope that Andy wore in a coil about his shoulders. I was a mountain climber now, and my pride as I trudged upward helped to counterbalance any doubts I had.

An hour later I was not so sure. There, a hundred feet away from me, sat Andy in the deep snow of a steep gully into which he had crossed. I had watched him inch his way over above a yawning void on what looked like miniscule holds, digging his ice axe in and cautiously transferring his weight from foot to foot.

Now it was my turn. Before, the rope had been above me, and its reassuring tug had kept my attention focused upward. Now, any tug from the rope would pull me off, and as I edged out toward him, my body pressed against the ice, I could not avoid seeing the drop to the valley below. It made my head spin and my stomach knot as snow displaced by my lumbering movements seemed to spiral forever downward.

A short way across I stuck. My hands scrabbled in the snow for a hold. I thrust my ice axe nervously into the soft powder, looking desperately for security. I could not go on. Encouraging noises came from Andy. No, I could not go on. But then I realized that I could not go back! Uncertain and frightened, I seemed to hang there for an age.

Then I made my decision and blundered on. At that moment the holds I was standing on collapsed and I was in space falling backward into the terrifying abyss. I swung at the snow with my ice axe, but to no avail. I continued to plummet downward.

Suddenly, with a jerk, the rope came tight and I lay panting on the snow. I was in one piece. No injuries. No blood. I still had my ice axe. The rope had held. My fear vanished and a feeling of great confidence washed over me. There was nothing to this climbing, then. I had fallen and swung about sixty feet and I felt great.

I quickly climbed back up to Andy and half jokingly offered to lead. Wisely, he said no. The rest of the climb was straightforward, and we reached the summit as the sun began to dip into the sea to the west. Before us row upon row of snow-clad peaks stretched to the horizon. Inside me great feelings of pride and humility welled up. I had never seen a sight so beautiful nor felt so deserving of it. My fall was forgotten and with it my clumsiness and my fear.

Within a month I knew several things about that first climb. By then I could have repeated it without a moment's anxiety, for it was, in truth, easy. But I had been lucky: firstly, at having ignored my mother who had insisted that if I was going to the mountains with Andy, we should not take a rope, since the presence of a rope would mean that we intended to leave the beaten trail for steeper slopes. Secondly, in having a companion who knew how to handle the rope when I fell; and thirdly, that the rope, an old hemp line that had been used to tow automobiles, had not broken.

The purpose of this book is to introduce aspiring climbers to the sport of mountaineering with its vast potential for joyous ex-perience. It will not make anyone a mountaineer. Only many days on mountains can do that. What it will try to do is provide the knowledge to help the novice do the correct things, make the right decisions, and use the equipment of the sport to its best advantage. If I had had such a book before my first climb, perhaps I would not have hugged the ice, or scrabbled at the holds, and had I fallen, I would have been able to stop myself quickly. Mountaineering has its dangers; they are a part of what makes the sport such a compelling pursuit. If this book does what it sets out to do, it will make you aware of the dangers and at the same time instruct in the correct techniques that can minimize them. For me, techniques are only a means to an end. The end is the joy of safe movement in the mountains; the unsurpassed pleasure of making the vertical world your home.

Chapter 1

THE DEVELOPMENT OF MOUNTAINEERING

Mountaineering encompasses several other sports because the ascent of a mountain involves a variety of techniques and pursuits. To get to the mountain may demand a considerable amount of walking over high passes and through rough country, including the crossing of wilderness rivers. Down from the mountain may sweep a glacier which has to be negotiated before one comes to grips with the steeper ridges and walls. On some mountains, as on Everest, for example, the traversing of the glacier and its icefalls may prove more difficult and dangerous than the route on the peak. Once on a mountain itself the ascent may include advanced use of rock-climbing and ice-climbing techniques. All these components of mountaineering require the development of particular skills and knowledge, and it is perhaps not surprising that they have developed into the status of separate sports.

Rock climbers, who have no desire to climb mountains but get their enjoyment out of the increasing technical difficulty of gymnastic moves on steep rock, can be found in Yosemite or the Shawangunks. The same is also true, but to a lesser extent, of ice climbers. The growing popularity of high-angle frozen waterfall climbing in the United States may lead to a growing group of devotees who rock climb in summer and ice climb in winter but do not ascend mountains. There is nothing inferior in this. Indeed, the abilities on high-angle rock sharpened, for example, in the competitive climate of Eldorado Canyon in Colorado, can be essential in the ascent of more serious routes in the high mountains. So, out of the pursuit of mountaineering have evolved the sports of backpacking, ice climbing, and rock climbing, some of the participants of which never attempt the ascent of a high mountain.

The motivation of the early pioneers was the ascent of unclimbed mountains, the wish to stand where no one had stood before. But in so doing, they discovered the utter joy of safe movement over difficult rock or ice and began to ascend these challenges for the sheer pleasure and adventure that they offered. Climbers, even if they are in an area where the rock has been climbed for a long time, can still experience the thrill of discovery. Imagination or technical ability can lead to the discovery of a new way up a cliff, and each winter gives a different configuration of the ice in the waterfalls and couloirs.

Whereas in Europe access to the high peaks was easy, in the nineteenth century in America many peaks remained inaccessible and virgin. For prospective mountaineers in the eastern states, a climbing season in the Swiss Alps was less difficult than an expedition to the Rockies or the Tetons. Consequently, American mountaineering lagged behind its European counterpart.

It was not until the growth of indus-

On Lost Arrow Spire, City of Rock, Idaho. (*R. Shaw*)

trialization and leisure in the 1930s that the standards of mountaineering in America began to rival those in Europe. The main mountain summits had fallen to the explorer. In the Tetons, Mount Owen, the last unclimbed peak, was ascended in 1930 when two rangers, Fryxell and Smith, of the newly formed Grand Teton National Park joined forces with two easterners, Underhill and Henderson, members of the Appalachian Mountain Club. Climbers now turned their attention to new and more difficult routes, and superb ascents of the faces and ridges of the Tetons were made by climbers like Durrance, Petzoldt, and Unsoeld.

In California the Sierra Club was responsible for fine climbs on Mount Whitney and in Yosemite. With the ascent of Higher Cathedral Spire in Yosemite Valley, the psychological breakthrough onto the steep and intimidating faces of the Valley heralded the development of modern rock climbing in the United States. But it was not until after the Second World War that the sport really became popular. The growing affluence that brought a car to most families, plus the increase in leisure time, and the lack of challenge in the urban environment made the mountains appealing. Moreover, cheap and easily available surplus equipment from the war brought the sport within reach of many.

Climbs like the ascent of Lost Arrow in Yosemite, California, by Salathe and Nelson in 1947, the Open Book by Royal Robbins at Tahquitz, California, in 1952, and the climbs of desert monoliths like Totem Pole, in Monument Valley, Utah, by Powell, Gallwas, and Wilson, in 1955 brought West Coast rock climbing to a new high standard. In the East the discovery and ascent of routes on the Shawangunks, New York State, by Fritz Weissner, in the 1940s, opened up a cliff within reach of the mountaineers of New York, and farther north the Cathedral Cliffs of New Hampshire attracted climbers from Quebec.

Colorado climbing in the forties and fifties did not reach the technical heights attained by the climbers in California or the eastern

United States. High standard rock climbing usually flourishes on readily accessible cliffs near to centers of population where climbers can make ascents in summer evenings or weekends without a long expedition to reach the cliff. In Colorado, many large mountains attracted the climber and interest was mainly focused on the ascent of obvious features rather than on routes of technical difficulty. A route on a mountain like Longs Peak took several days and much organization to accomplish. A climber making ascents in say, Yosemite, California, would in the same time climb a much greater height of difficult rock, and the competition to climb harder new routes in a more compact area like Yosemite was much more intense. A group of young climbers led by Layton Kor, in the late 1950s, soon changed that situation. The great rock climbing of Eldorado and Boulder Canyons close to Boulder and Denver began to be opened up, and on the high mountains, Kor and Northcutt were responsible for the ascent of the Diagonal Route on Longs Peak, in 1959, which was a major advance in difficulty, for a high mountain climb.

The 1960s saw a period when the isolation of climbers in different centers, from developments elsewhere, began to be broken down due to greater affluence. Climbers began to travel more widely. Expeditions to Alaska and the Andes became more common, and the Bugaboos in Canada attracted a large number of climbers from all over America, including Fred Beckey, that most ubiquitous of mountaineers.

Later, the move was to larger faces where objective dangers were greater than on the regular routes. The year 1961 saw the ascent of Willis Wall on Mount Rainier, the Black Ice Couloir on the Grand Teton, and most impressive, the climb by Chouinard, Beckey, and Doody of the north face of Mount Edith Cavell in Alberta, Canada. These climbs were of a high technical difficulty on large mountains and involved good organization and sustained skill.

Mountaineering has rapidly become an in-

The Bastille, a superb cliff with testing routes in Eldorado Canyon, near Boulder, Colorado. (*R. Shaw*)

ternational pursuit. American climbers have made their mark in the European Alps, and European mountaineers have been responsible for new difficult ascents in North America. This interchange has led to increases in technical ability and to great improvement in the equipment available to climbers, as climbers learned of new techniques from each other. The modern climber is likely to be equipped with boots from France, crampons from California, rope from Switzerland, ice axes from Scotland, chocks from Colorado, and carabiners from Austria.

The trend in climbing has gone from an extensive use of pitons and bolts toward "clean climbing." Ten years ago in Yosemite no party set out for the faces without pounds of hardware clanking around them, but now pitons have been replaced by chocks which slot neatly and silently into cracks and can be removed again without damage. This development, pioneered by British climbers, has been taken up eagerly by North Americans, and the standards of free climbing that is, climbing with the least possible assistance from technological aids, have been pushed to new limits.

New challenges abound. In recent years there has been a growth in winter climbing with the ascent of routes under a cloak of snow and ice, which were ascended formerly only with difficulty in summer conditions. Advances in equipment developed by Yvon Chouinard have made the ascent of many ice-covered rock climbs and frozen waterfalls feasible.

Another noticeable development in mountaineering is the growth of participation in the sport by women. Until recently women have rarely performed in such numbers, or with such drive and ability as men. While still outnumbered, women have nevertheless advanced to the forefront in the sport. Now women set out, not with male companions but partnered by other women, to climb routes that would have defeated the elite of male climbers only a few years ago. The year 1973 saw an all-woman ascent of El Capitan by Beverly Johnson and Sybille Hechtel, and female teams have made difficult ascents on Mount McKinley and in the Tetons, and on Himalayan peaks such as Annapurna.

Mountaineering is an individualistic pursuit, and its history is one of independence and daring. Despite the growth in numbers of those taking part in the sport, many unexplored mountain ranges and faces still offer solitude and demand skill. Mountaineering is a sport where the novice faces the same problems as the expert and receives the same measure of satisfaction. Mountains are never conquered; only our own failings are defeated during the ascent.

Chapter 2

THE MAIN FEATURES OF MOUNTAINS AND ROCK FACES

Mountaineering is an international sport, and the names for the common features of mountains and rock faces reflect this. Some terms are peculiar to certain countries. For example, a *dihedral,* the name used in North America for an open-book corner, a rock feature where two faces intersect like a standing open book, would be referred to in Britain as a *corner* and in Europe as a *diedre.* Some of the names used are interchangeable and imprecise. A cleft splitting a face may be called a *gully* or a *couloir,* or even on occasion a *chimney;* a *col* may also be known as a *pass, a notch,* or a *saddle.* Within a particular area, the terms usually have a more precise meaning. The names for some mountain features are also used to denote similar, but much smaller components of a rock face. Thus, a *wall* can mean a section of very steep rock maybe fifty feet in height, or the three-thousand-foot face of El Capitan.

THE MAIN FEATURES OF MOUNTAINS

(1) *Bergshrund* This is the very large crevasse found between a snowfield and the rock face, or at the point where a snowfield joins a glacier. Late in the season when snow-bridges have collapsed, crossing the bergshrund may prove difficult.

(2) *Buttress* A part of the mountain, usually rock, projecting from the main mass. This feature may also be called a *spur* or a *nose.*

(3) *Col* A dip in a ridge between two peaks. If the gap is a broad one, it is often called a *pass* or a *saddle;* if it is narrow it may be referred to as a *notch.*

(4) *Cornice* A wind-formed overhang of snow at the head of a couloir, or along the edges of a snow ridge. Cornices can become extremely unstable and are a major hazard on an approach from below or the traverse of a ridge. When they are stable they can occasionally be surmounted by tunneling.

(5) *Couloir* A fairly wide gully or cleft on a mountain, which is often steep in its upper section. A couloir acts as a funnel for falling snow and rock, but often provides a good route of ascent to the summit.

(6) *Crevasse* A split in a glacier caused by the movement of the ice. In general, crevasses run across the glacier. They may be crossed, usually in winter or early spring, by snow bridges.

(7) *Face* A large relatively unbroken and steep aspect of a mountain, defined by two adjacent ridges. A face may also be referred to as a *wall* or *cliff.* Many classic mountaineering routes ascend faces. North faces, which are subject to the most severe weather, often pro-

The main features of a mountain. (*J. Shaw*)

vide considerable challenges, demanding first-class technique on rock and ice.

(8) *Glacier* A river of ice, often snow-covered in its upper reaches, moving slowly from the peak to the valley. A steep glacier or one that is forced through a narrowing of its valley may be heavily crevassed. Directions are given on a glacier as though one were looking down it, in the direction of flow of the glacier.

(9) *Hanging Glacier* A steep glacier that is separated from the main glacier below by a cliff of rock or ice.

(10) *Icefall* A chaotic section of the glacier with many crevasses and *seracs* caused by the steepening of the glacier over a cliff. Due to the unstable nature of the ice and its relatively more rapid movement, icefalls are serious obstacles.

(11) *Lateral Moraine* The debris left by a glacier on its banks. It consists usually of fairly unstable *talus*.

(12) *Notch* A narrow gap or col on a ridge.

(13) *Ridge* A sharp buttress running from the summit. Often several summits will be joined by a ridge. Ridges provide routes that are least subject to the hazards of rockfall and avalanche. A feature of ridges is pinnacles or gendarmes, which are rock towers. The ascent and descent of these rock formations may make even a short ridge a lengthy route.

(14) *Rognon* A small wedge of rock protruding through a glacier or snowfield. Often a rognon provides a safe haven on a glacier subject to rockfall or avalanche.

(15) *Serac* A pinnacle or face of ice in the icefall of a glacier. Seracs are often unstable and may fall due to the movement of the glacier or melting caused by the sun.

(16) *Summit* The highest point of a peak.

(17) *Terminal Moraine* The debris deposited at the end of a glacier.

(18) *Wall* A large, steep face of a mountain.

THE MAIN FEATURES OF A ROCK FACE

(1) *Arete* A sharp, well-defined ridge.

(2) *Bulge* An area of rock that exceeds the vertical, usually for a small distance.

(3) *Chimney* A cleft in the rock where it is possible to insert the body and proceed, using both walls of the cleft.

(4) *Crack* A narrow split in the rock, varying in width from one where thin pitons can be inserted to a fissure that almost permits the entry of the climber.

(5) *Dihedral* An open-book corner, frequently a crack at the junction of the two faces. This feature is also called a corner or a diedre.

(6) *Gangway* An upward-slanting ledge that often leads across a steep face of rock.

(7) *Groove* A narrow depression in a face, often lacking a usable crack.

(8) *Gully* A deep and wide cleft, usually formed by water or ice action. The steepness

The main features of a rock face. (*J. Shaw*)

of a gully is rarely continuous, and pitches of rock are often separated by large ledges or less-steep sections.

(9)   *Ledge*   A more or less horizontal section of rock protruding from a face.

(10)   *Overhang*   A section of rock exceeding the vertical, for a greater distance than a bulge.

(11)   *Pinnacle*   A tower of rock separated from the main mass, sometimes called a gendarme when it occurs on a ridge.

(12)   *Rib*   A small and less sharply defined arete or ridge.

(13)   *Roof*   An overhang that protrudes horizontally from the rock face. It is also called a ceiling.

(14)   *Slab*   A section of rock angled between about 30 and 70 degrees. The rock is often more water-worn and smoother than other features of the face.

(15)   *Talus*   A mass of broken rock, usually found below, or on a less-steep section of a cliff. Another name for this is *scree*.

(16)   *Wall*   A steep and continuous section of rock, usually exceeding 70 degrees in angle. See also *Face* under Main Features of Mountains.

Chapter 3

A GLOSSARY OF COMMON CLIMBING TERMS

Climbing, like most sports, has a language of its own. Ask a climber whether he enjoyed the climb he has just finished and you may, if you are not familiar with the language, be bemused and confused by the answer.

"Great," he may say. "The crux was a real beauty. About five-nine. You have to lean way out on a pinch hold, and get a poor jam just above the bulge. Then you swing into a layback on the edge. There's a good chock runner just below, but you need a long sling on the carabiner, or, when you get on the delicate mantelshelf above the bulge, the drag'll be too much." And so on.

This would not be a deliberate attempt to confuse you with jargon, but a desire to communicate, as fully as possible, the techniques and equipment used on the climb and the difficulties encountered. To be able to discuss in detail a particular climb is part of the enjoyment of the sport for most climbers.

Here then is a glossary of climbing terms in most common use. As with descriptive mountain and rock-face terms, you will find some variation from one climbing area to the next, but the differences will be slight.

Aid Climbing The ascent of a face using pitons or bolts driven into the rock, on which are hung stirrups to provide holds.

Bandolier A loop of rope or tape worn around the body on which is hung slings, carabiners, and chocks, stacked to allow easy selection.

Belay A position where a climber is secured to the rock and can, without being pulled from the rock, bring up the second or safeguard the leader, in the event of a fall.

Bivouac An improvised camp made with limited equipment.

Carabiner A metal loop with a spring gate through which the rope can be passed, to make a belay or a running belay. The spring gate enables the climber's rope to be passed into the carabiner without untying the rope.

Chimney A technique used to ascend a wide crack where the back is moved up one wall and the feet or knees up the other.

Chock A piece of metal that can be wedged into a crack and to which a sling of rope, tape, or wire is attached.

Clean Climbing The ascent of a climb without the use of pitons or bolts to assist progress. Also called free climbing.

Crampon An arrangement of metal spikes strapped to the sole of the boot for climbing ice.

Crux The most difficult pitch or series of moves of an ascent.

Edging Using the sides of the boot on small, usually sharp, holds.

Cathedral Peak, Yosemite, California. (*R. Shaw*)

Fingerhold   A small hold that will accommodate only the tips of the fingers.

Glissade   A controlled snow slide used as a method of descent.

Grade   The difficulty of a climb described by some agreed method. There are several different systems of grading or rating. The British use an adjectival system, e.g., very severe, whereas the favored American system is numerical, e.g., 5.7, on an open-ended scale of 5.1 upward to, at present, 5.12.

Hand Traverse   A technique where the climber moves across a section of steep rock by hanging from handholds.

Hold   An irregularity on the rock face that the hand or foot can use to assist progress.

Jamming   A technique where the body or part of the body is wedged in a crack.

Jug Handle   A large hold with a sharp edge around which the fingers can curl.

Layback   A technique where the climber ascends a corner by walking the feet up holdless rock, while leaning back on the edge of a crack.

Mantelshelf   A technique by which the climber levers himself onto a ledge, usually without the benefit of footholds below it or handholds above.

Natural Protection   Protection afforded by features of the rock, such as chockstones and rock spikes, to which runners can be attached.

Objective Danger   A risk factor not within the climber's control such as weather, rockfall, avalanche, etc.

Pinch Hold   A feature of the rock that can be held on to by using the pressure of the fingers and thumb.

Pitch   A section of a rock climb between two belaying positions.

Protection   A runner or series of runners that can be arranged on the pitch to safeguard the leader.

Prusik Loop or Sling   A sling attached to a hanging rope with a knot that will allow the sling to slide on the rope unless the climber's weight is on the sling.

Rappel   A method of descending a cliff using the friction of the rope around the body of the climber, or through a special device, such as a Figure 8 descending device, to take the weight of the climber.

Running Belay or Runner   Protection fixed on a pitch by the leader. The rope is run through a carabiner on a sling that is attached to some natural feature of the rock or to a chock, piton, or bolt.

Self-Arrest   The technique of stopping a slide on snow or ice using the pick of the ice axe.

Serious Ascent   A climb on which there are objective dangers or a lack of protection.

Sling   A sling is a short, say 5-foot length of rope, tape, or wire tied in such a way as to form a continuous loop. It is used to hang over projections or is threaded behind a chockstone to enable the climber to secure himself to the rock. A rope sling can be used as a prusik loop.

Stemming or Bridging   A technique used in a corner or crack where footholds are found on opposite walls.

Step Cutting   The action of hewing small platforms on snow and ice to allow the climber to ascend or descend.

Technical Difficulty   The hardness of a particular move or series of moves.

Tension Traverse   A traverse made, in the absence of adequate holds, by moving against the pull of the rope.

Traverse
1. A more or less horizontal series of moves.
2. The ascent and descent of a peak by different routes.
3. A route following a ridge, linking peaks.

Undercling   A hold that is used with the palm of the hand upward.

Chapter 4

INTERLUDE: HIGH TRAVERSE, CHAMONIX, FRANCE

The morning was bright and clear and the blue of the sky seemed almost black over the intense white of the ridge. Before us it stretched toward the horizon, broad at first, then narrowing to a knife edge of rock and snow, eventually to lose itself in a chaotic cluster of sharp peaks. Below, the town of Chamonix was beginning to bustle into motion and the sunlight glinted off the automobiles hurrying toward the Mont Blanc Tunnel.

Up here we were in a different world, the air clean and invigorating, and the only sounds the crunch of our crampons in the snow. We had made a rather late start, and we moved quickly on the ridge carrying coils of rope in our hands, ready to check a fall should a slip occur.

Bill and Ted went ahead and Jennifer and I followed. We were all heavily laden since we carried food and equipment for an extended stay at the end of the ridge.

It was not long before the ridge narrowed and we began to move one at a time to negotiate the gendarmes which barred the way. The first one was a monolith of rough granite split by a crack the width of a boot. Up I went, revelling in the warmth of the rock, securely jamming my boot in the crack and feeling in its recesses for sharp holds. Where no hold existed, I braced my hand across the walls of the crack and moved up. The crack went

quickly and soon I was sitting on a ledge, looking back toward the fairy-tale castle of the Aiguille de Midi as I ran the rope round my waist to Jennifer. Soon she joined me and we traversed round the summit of the gendarme to regain the ridge. At this point it was sharp, and steep slopes fell away to the north and south. The sun was already beginning to soften the snow and our boots were sinking into the crust. We pressed on, moving between obstacles as quickly as our loads allowed. Sometimes we bypassed the towers of rock on the north side above Chamonix, and there the ice was rock hard. Chips of ice flew out as I swung my axe, cutting steps across the steep slope that dropped for two thousand feet to the glacier below. The ridge in places was heavily corniced. The wind had sculpted the snow into a great curve that swung back into an overhang sometimes ten feet in extent. A cornice like this can easily fracture, especially in the heat of the afternoon, and we tried to keep well clear.

At one point the ridge became bare rock and so narrow that there was room only for one foot placed carefully after the other. Sometimes I have negotiated a very sharp ridge like this, by inching along on the seat of my pants, one leg hanging down each side. That day, it was exhilarating to balance on our feet in safety over the drop.

(R. Shaw)

As we reached our objective, the Aiguille de Plan, the weather began to deteriorate with black clouds sweeping in from the west. Storms in the mountains can be extremely dangerous, and our enjoyment of the climb had led us to ignore the signs of the changing sky. Now we hastened to descend off the ridge to the comfort and safety of the hut. There was still a long descent before we would reach it, and the glacier we had to go down was unknown to all of us. Our two companions were on their first major route and had never before been on a difficult glacier.

From the lowest point of the ridge we began to rappel about a hundred and fifty feet down to the bergshrund, the crevasse where the rock and ice meet. Snowflakes began to fall in ever increasing flurries and, back above the Midi, a flash of lightning and the accompanying crash of thunder made our descent more urgent.

I placed a loop of rope around a good spike of rock, doubled the rope and threw it out into space. Then, with another rope, I belayed myself and began to safeguard the descent of the others. One by one they disappeared into the gloom with the rappel rope around them and the safety rope attached by a bowline to their waist. Jennifer was the last one down and, when she reached the snow, I rappelled down to join them.

Once over the edge the rope hung free for most of its length and I descended, gyrating slowly.

Another flash of lightning and the unearthly boom of thunder echoing round the walls of granite made us move fast. Too fast. As I coiled the safety rope, Ted pulled on one end of the rappel rope to bring it through the loop and down to us. When he got to the point where it ought to have dropped, the rope jammed at the loop a hundred and fifty feet above us. The urgency of our situation had made him pull the rope without checking that

(R. Shaw)

(R. Shaw)

no knots or tangles were present. We tugged and heaved but it would not budge. I made a feeble attempt to climb back up the rock, but it was too steep and the falling snow did not encourage me. With the help of the hanging rope I might have succeeded but to have used it would have been extremely foolish as it could have released at any moment.

Returning to the others, I thought for a moment, then cut the rope with an ice axe. We needed the rope for the steep glacier ahead and for a five-hundred-foot rock step above the hut. So, tied to the rope, which was now half its former three hundred feet, Jennifer and I followed Ted and Bill across the edge of the bergshrund. Between us and the rock was a deep, wide cleft, while to our right the glacier fell in a steep cliff for a hundred feet or so. We moved cautiously but together since

darkness was approaching and we wanted to be off the glacier before the light went. Below us we could see that the glacier was very broken with many crevasses that would make our descent time consuming.

Suddenly, from Jennifer behind me, I heard a shout and jerked round to see her falling backward down the slope. The edge she had been moving on had collapsed.

I drove my axe into the snow as deep as I could, passed the rope round the shaft, and dropped with my knee on top of the head. Jennifer was using her axe in the ice to slow her fall and the jerk when it came on the rope was not too severe. The belay held, and Jennifer climbed up the steep ice to rejoin me. We smiled at each other and then continued.

It was not to be her lucky day. Half an hour later, in the dwindling light, a snowbridge

(*J. Shaw*)

over a large crevasse that she was crossing partly collapsed and she was left, wedged at the waist, with her legs in space. The only remedy was to dig away around herself until she could mantelshelf back up on to the remains of the bridge. A nerve-wracking operation.

We threaded our way down the glacier, zigzagging to circumvent the deep crevasses, sometimes crossing them on shaky snowbridges, sometimes jumping over them in a heart-stopping leap. It was dark by the time we reached the rock step, and as none of us felt enthusiastic about its descent in the dark and the snow, we found a spacious ledge, overhung above, and made ourselves as comfortable as possible. Soon the stove was roaring, melting snow, and we huddled together in our sleeping bags, drinking hot soup and chatting about the excitements and joys of the day.

Outside, the snow blanketed everything, while under the overhang only a few flakes swirled onto our faces. Beyond the bivouac was the cold, icy world, but here we were warmed by our companionship and the shared pleasures of the climb. We had made mistakes, we had been slow, we had had accidents, but we had done what we set out to do and had enjoyed it immensely. And we had each learned something from the experience; the necessity of starting early on a major climb, the need to be methodical with the organization and dismantling of rappels, the importance of knowing the abilities of your companions in the high mountains, and the lesson that vigilance and concentration are vital from one's departure to one's safe return.

Chapter 5

CLOTHING AND EQUIPMENT FOR THE CLIMBER

The first essential piece of equipment for a climber is a good pair of boots. A climber moves on his feet, and it is important that you feel confident in the ability of your boots to grip the rock. The difference between the feel of a well-fitting pair of boots designed for rock climbing and an old pair of walking boots is astonishing. However, if you have walking boots, try them out on a few climbs until you have enough experience to decide

A selection of mountaineering boots suitable for rock climbing, walking, and summer low-altitude mountaineering. Knickers allow free movement of the legs. (*Courtesy, Recreational Equipment, Inc.*)

what you are looking for in climbing boots. The most modern equipment is not essential in climbing, it just makes life so much easier. The ideal in a pair of boots would be ones that enable you to walk in on the long trail to the peak in comfort, and then would be close fitting and rigid enough to enable you to stand at ease on very small holds on a steep face. But, like so many other ideals, this one is unavailable.

I have had about fifteen pairs of boots in my life. None of them was ever perfect. Some were superb hiking boots that gobbled up the miles, but felt like diving boots on steep slabs; others seemed to possess guidance systems on small holds, but blistered my heels and toes on the long walk in. Compromise is the name of the game. Choose boots that fit snugly but comfortably and do not have an entirely rigid sole. If you intend to climb in winter, you will need boots that go over two pairs of socks. I once had a pair of boots that were ideal in the summer but in winter on a difficult climb, where my movements were slow, they so constricted my feet that I lost the feeling in my toes for about a month and narrowly escaped the more serious effects of frostbite.

In a later chapter I'll come back to winter and ice-climbing equipment, but for the moment what you need is a good pair of general mountaineering boots such as the Raichle Aletsch or Robson, or one of the Galibier range, such as the Peuterey, or my favorite, the Super Guide. A pair of short gaiters to keep the feet dry and to prevent the entry of small stones is also good to have.

Boot choice is not something one can be dogmatic about. What you will be looking for is a reasonably stiff sole incorporating a metal shank. The sole of the boot should have a very small welt to enable your foot to fit snugly onto the smallest holds when you are edging. The best lacing pattern is one that uses D rings for about half the length of the boot, topped by hooks. Go into a climbing store and ask to see their range of boots. Take plenty of time in your choice and be sure to wear the socks that you would on the mountain. Don't be rushed in your choice; your feet are the most important technical aids in mountaineering.

Well-designed boots for mountaineering and rock climbing. (*Courtesy, Recreational Equipment, Inc.*)

Short gaiters are useful in keeping feet dry and blocking the entry of small stones. (*Courtesy, Forrest Mountaineering*)

Good wool socks are helpful in the prevention of blisters. (*Courtesy, Forrest Mountaineering*)

If you are going to do a lot of rock climbing on easily accessible cliffs like those of Yosemite or the Canyons of Colorado or Utah, or in the eastern states, you will want a pair of specialized rock-climbing boots. These are lightweight boots with canvas uppers and a smooth, stiff, black-rubber sole. Some climbers prefer a lightweight boot with a vibram sole. This boot is sometimes called a Kletter-shoe. An American example of it is the Royal Robbins Yosemite boot or the "Shoenard" made by Chouinard. Most climbers, however, prefer the smooth-soled, lightweight climbing boot, though it does make the descent of steep

Modern rock-climbing boots give an excellent grip on small holds. (*R. Shaw*)

trails after the climb more hazardous. The most popular type is the E.B., a French-made, technical climbing, lightweight boot. Other very similar boots are the Pierre Allain and the René Desmaison rock-climbing boots made by Galibier.

The advice on choosing mountain boots applies equally well to rock boots. Take your time, try several types, and make sure you get a good fit.

When I bought my first pair of rock boots, the fashion was to have them very tight fitting. In the store they seemed fine but once on the rock I discovered that they had their problems. The security they gave on steep rock was amazing, but, if the pitch was a long one, I found that the pain in my feet became more and more distracting. My first action on reaching a ledge was not to belay; it was to remove the boots from my screaming feet. So, buy your boots snug, but not crippling.

The problem with lightweight rock-climbing boots is that they are so pleasant to climb in. One feels really light-footed, the friction is superb, and all one's movements seem graceful. Consequently, it is difficult to persuade oneself to climb in heavy boots. Yet on mountains, boots are what you will be wearing. So it is important to use them in practice situations and develop the different techniques and attitudes they demand, so that on the high mountains you feel at home in them.

Obviously, the clothing you will need will depend on the mountain you are going to climb and the time of year. What would be adequate for Shiprock in New Mexico, where temperatures are always high, would be reckless on the Grand Teton in Wyoming. The clothing I will describe would be suitable for severe conditions on the high peaks. Most climbers favor warm wool climbing knickers for big mountains. They give considerably greater freedom of movement than ordinary pants and will retain much of their insulation even if wet. Jeans are dangerous for mountain wear as denim provides low insulation, even when dry. On lower altitude climbs, though many climbers wear them, they are restricting

and obscure the view of the holds on steep rock, as they extend over the top of the boot.

Above the waist a string vest is a useful item, as it traps a layer of air next to the body and also prevents perspiration from soaking the shirt. Over the string vest I favor a wool shirt with a long tail to tuck into my pants.

A good, thick wool sweater, not too tight at the neck, is essential. Wool has the important advantage that when it is wet it is still capable of reducing the heat loss from the body. This is not true of synthetic fibers.

Topping this, you will need a good windproof parka with a well-designed hood that

A waterproof parka is essential equipment on a mountain. One that opens completely prevents overheating. This parka incorporates a hood that tucks away below the collar. (*Courtesy, Nevisport*)

does not constrict head movement, but can fit snugly around the face in a storm. Suitable parkas abound. Among the best are the Sierra Design 60/40 Parka, the Camp 7 Mountain Parka, or the Kelty Windstopper. Make sure that you buy your parka large enough to fit over warm clothing and still allow you to move.

Protection of the head is very important, and all climbers should possess and use a climbing helmet. Since their introduction, helmets have saved a large number of lives. A friend of mine once fell with his companion while we were all on a serious winter ascent. When my partner and I climbed down to where they had fallen six hundred feet below, Martin's helmet was very badly smashed, but he was conscious and not seriously hurt. Of course, when the sun is beating down on Eldorado Canyon or Yosemite Valley and everyone is in shorts, you will not see many climbers wearing helmets; nevertheless, they are increasing the risk of the sport considerably. In the high mountains, with the increased danger of rockfall, a helmet is essential.

A great variety of helmets is offered for sale. Some are of poor quality. The American National Standards Institute had laid down standards for industrial use, but no standard exists at present for climbing helmets. Perhaps the best guide is the series of tests carried out by Mountain Safety Research of Seattle, Washington. Their helmet, the M.S.R., though expensive, is of a superior design. Another good design is the Joe Brown, imported from Wales.

The lifeline of mountaineers, the rope, is the item of equipment that makes the sport possible and prevents it from being a foolhardy pursuit. Rope development has taken great strides in recent years. At one time all climbers used a natural-fiber rope of low strength, poor handling, and short life. Then the nylon rope was introduced and became universally used. These ropes were made of continuous filaments with a tight lay. This kind of rope is called Goldline. In recent

This harness is light and comfortable. It has removable and adjustable equipment loops for climbers who prefer to carry carabiners, chocks and other gear from the waist. The rope is attached to the harness with a bowline or a figure-eight knot. (*D. Van Pelt. Courtesy, Forrest Mountaineering*)

years, it has been largely superseded by perlon Kernmantle ropes consisting of an inner braided or twisted core surrounded by a sheath of cross-braided continuous filaments. The Kernmantle rope is much more pleasant to handle, does not kink so easily, and has much less stretch with low loads than the Goldline-type rope.

The International Alpine Association (UIAA) subjects ropes to a standardized series of tests and gives their seal of approval if the rope meets their standards. The test demands that a climbing rope sustaining a fall of 176 pounds through a distance of 16.4 feet should put a maximum impact on the climber of no more than 2,640 pounds, the remainder of the energy being absorbed by the elasticity of the rope. It also calls for the rope to do this

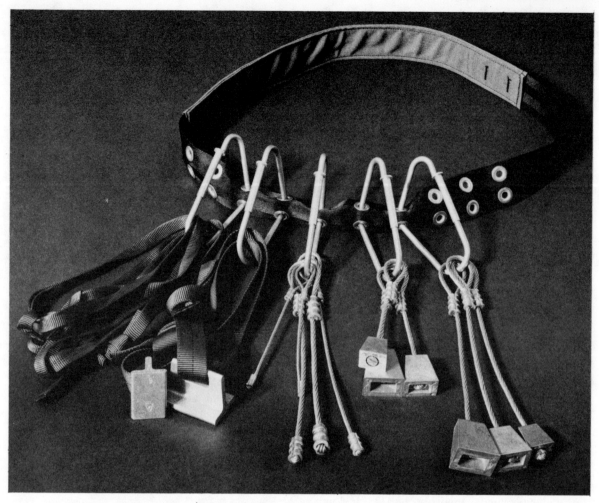

A gear sling or bandolier fitted with pin bins. These enable the climber to select the correct sling or chock without difficulty. (*D. Van Pelt. Courtesy, Forrest Mountaineering*)

three times without breaking. You should always buy a rope that meets UIAA approval. Among the trade names of such ropes are Edelrid, Mammut Edelweiss, and Rocca. In my opinion the latter, retailed by Forrest Mountaineering, is the superior rope. Most climbers use an 11mm single rope of 150 feet for rock climbing, and a 9mm rope, of the same length, on a mountain to give longer rappels.

The rope must always be treated very carefully and when not in use stored in a cool, dry place away from acids and solvents. When climbing, always take care not to stand on the rope or to put pressure on it over a sharp edge. Check the rope frequently for fraying and retire it immediately if it is severely damaged, or if it has sustained several leader falls. The expense of good equipment is minimal compared to that of hospitalization. Another recent development in mountaineering is the use of a body harness. At one time climbers tied on to the rope using a bowline knot, and many still do. The problem is that if a fall occurs the shock load is transferred to the climber on the single strand of rope around the waist and can cause internal damage. Moreover, if the climber ends up hanging in

Tube chocks from four to six inches in length and two and half inches in diameter to provide protection in wide jam cracks. (*Courtesy, The Great Pacific Iron Works*)

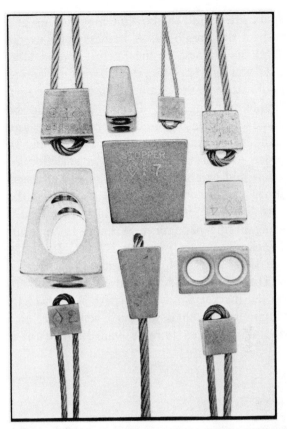

A selection of wedge-shaped stopper chocks which can be used with strong wire or perlon slings. (*Courtesy, The Great Pacific Iron Works*)

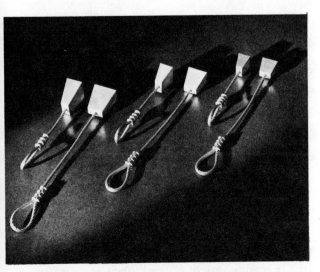

Foxhead chocks mounted on a single wire.
(*D. Van Pelt. Courtesy, Forrest Mountaineering*)

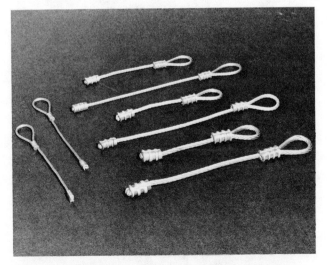

For very thin cracks, these Copperheads are ideal.
(*D. Van Pelt. Courtesy, Forrest Mountaineering*)

space after a fall the bowline may ride up and restrict the breathing. A harness such as the Whillans Harness or the Forrest Swami Harness will prevent this, though neither are as unobtrusive to the climber as the bowline or a simple webbing belt. The choice should be made taking into consideration the type and standard of climbing you intend to pursue. In order to belay you will need a selection of slings and carabiners. Most climbers now use slings made of nylon webbing, buy it by the yard, and tie it up into slings themselves, using a ring bend or tape knot. In general, 1-inch flat-weave webbing is best. It has a breaking strain of 4,000 pounds.

There is a bewildering variety of carabiners on the market. I use two types: a lightweight aluminum carabiner without a screwgate, and one of stronger chrome vanadium with a screwgate. The first, which has a strength of 4,000 pounds, only weighs about 2 ounces and can be carried in quantity for use on runners. The other type, which has a breaking strain of about 10,000 pounds, is used for belaying and for a rappel. I carry around ten of the first type and three of the latter.

Another essential for the modern climber is a wide selection of chocks or nuts. My advice is to acquire only a small number at first and buy additional ones as you gain experience. It is a mistake to load yourself down with too many. I have seen a climber at the beginning of a seventy-foot climb carrying about twenty chocks (yet good natural protection was available on the climb) while the climbers who made the first ascent used clumsy nailed boots and no runners. There is such a thing as overprotection, and like so many comforts, we can

The Titon is a very versatile chock and can be used in a wide variety of crack placements, often where a conventional chock would be useless. (*D. Hall. Courtesy, Forrest Mountaineering*)

come to rely too much on good runners so that where none is available, we feel naked.

Go into your climbing store and look at their selection, or send for a catalogue such as the excellent one produced by Forrest Mountaineering of Denver, Colorado, which has very good illustrations of the use of chocks. Probably about ten chocks is a large-enough number to start with, made up of some Foxhead wedges, Copperheads, Hexentic nuts, and one or two Titons. Once you have bought them go out to your local boulder and practice placing them in cracks, until you develop an instinct for the best jams.

Most climbers make use of a small backpack to carry equipment to the foot of the cliff, and to take with them if the climb is a long one. The pack is essential in the mountains, as there you will need a reserve of food and clothing and a supply of liquid. Moreover, on a mountain, it is an advantage to have a place to stow the ice axe and crampons when they are not in use.

Possibly the best packs in the United States are made by Lowe Alpine Systems. Their Alpine Pack is an excellent all-round medium-sized pack with provision for fixing crampons and an ice axe. Another well-tried pack is the Joe Brown from Karrimor of Britain, available through International Mountaineering Equipment, Inc.

Lastly, another piece of equipment that most climbers consider essential is a guidebook. These usually cover the most popular climbing areas and can be obtained from outdoor sports stores and some book shops.

In areas where guidebooks exist for the climbs, the difficulty of each climb is indicated

The Dougal Haston sack is an example of a good general-purpose mountaineering pack with fixings for crampons and ice axe. The bag can be used to give protection during an enforced bivouac. (*Courtesy, Nevisport*)

A haul sack designed for use on steep multi-day technical face climbs. (*D. Van Pelt. Courtesy, Forrest Mountaineering*)

A hammock enables a bivouac to be made on an overhanging wall. (*D. Hall. Courtesy, Forrest Mountaineering*)

by a rating of the climb. The system used varies from country to country and even from area to area in the United States. The most popular rating system for rock climbs in North America is the Decimal System. First developed at Tahquitz Rock in California it designated the difficulty of a climb on a scale of severity from 0–9. It was used to provide further information to the existing 6-point scale devised for the Sierras. In the 6-point scale, grades 1 through 3 were for ascents not requiring a rope. On grade-4 climbs, a rope was required and used to belay. Grade 5 was reserved for hard rock climbing where pitons would be used for protection, while grade 6 referred to aid climbing where progress was made in stirrups or pitons. The Decimal System subdivides the grade 5. Originally the degree of difficulty ranged from 5.0–5.9. Now the frontiers have been extended to 5.12, so the system is no longer a decimal one, and no doubt will be pushed yet farther in the future.

All guidebooks give an explanation of the system they use and, usually, a graded list of climbs, from the easiest to the most difficult, which is useful to the newcomer to the area.

Chapter 6

IMPORTANT KNOTS FOR MOUNTAINEERING

A mountaineer's life depends on the rope. The qualities that should be looked for in a climbing rope have already been discussed. Of equal importance are the knots that are used.

All knots weaken the strength of a rope. In general, the more acute the bend the rope makes within the knot, the more it is weakened. A small number of knots will cover most situations in mountaineering. These knots are described and illustrated in this chapter. However, I recommend that you get to know as many knots as possible. Unusual situations often occur, and the best way to deal with them may be by using an uncommon knot.

The Bowline This knot, which, like many others originated in sailing vessels, is traditionally the knot that is used to tie on to the end of the rope. Its main quality is that it produces a loop of rope that will not tighten under strain. Nowadays, with the growing popularity of climbing harnesses, it is less used. However, it is still used with some harnesses, like the Whillan's, and is an extremely useful knot to be familiar with.

Normally it is tied by passing the rope around the waist, with the short end in the right hand. A small loop is formed in the long end of the rope near the waist. The short end of the rope is passed through the loop, round the long end of the rope, and back down through the loop. The knot is adjusted until

it is tight against the waist. The short end of the rope is then secured by one or two half hitches. The half hitches are essential as, in nylon rope, it is possible for the bowline to work loose.

Double Figure Eight This knot also forms a non-slip loop and can be tied at any point in the rope. It is very useful for attaching the climbing rope to a carabiner, either when belaying or in conjunction with a body harness. In use, it is similar to the double overhand knot, but, since an additional twist is made in the knot, it is much easier to undo once strain has been put on it.

The knot is tied by taking a bend of the rope, passing it around the rope to form a loop, and passing the bend down through the loop. The loop of rope formed by this knot can be of any size. A small loop can be clipped into a carabiner. A larger loop can be formed, say, in the middle of the rope, and used to attach a third climber.

Ring Bend This knot, sometimes called the *overhand bend,* or the *tape knot,* is a simple, neat and effective way of joining the ends of a piece of web tape together, to form a loop that can be used as a sling.

First, an overhand knot is tied loosely in one end of the piece of tape. Then the other end is taken through the turns of the overhand so that both ends lie neatly against each other and point in opposite directions. With this

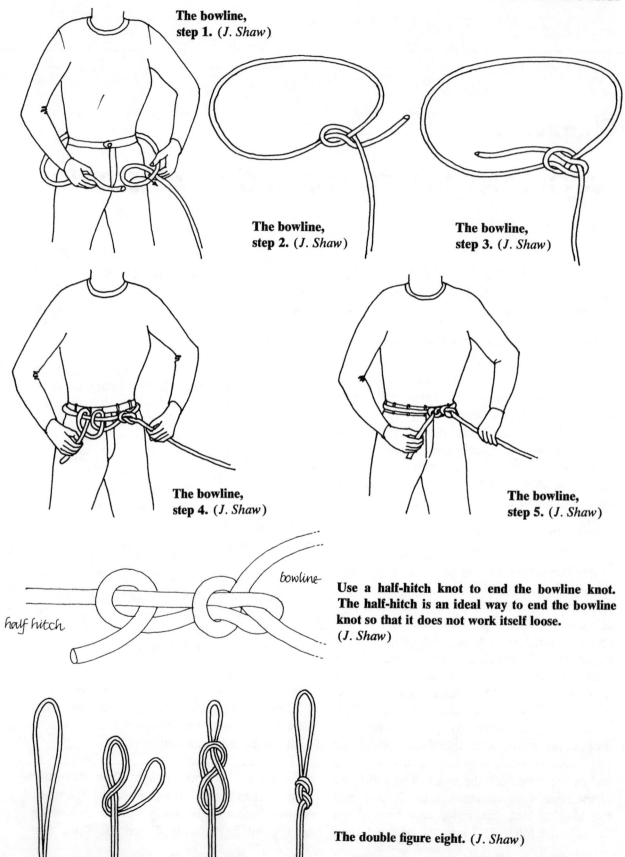

The bowline, step 1. (*J. Shaw*)

The bowline, step 2. (*J. Shaw*)

The bowline, step 3. (*J. Shaw*)

The bowline, step 4. (*J. Shaw*)

The bowline, step 5. (*J. Shaw*)

half hitch   bowline

Use a half-hitch knot to end the bowline knot. The half-hitch is an ideal way to end the bowline knot so that it does not work itself loose. (*J. Shaw*)

The double figure eight. (*J. Shaw*)

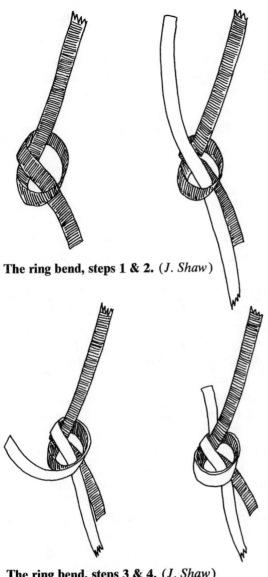

The ring bend, steps 1 & 2. (*J. Shaw*)

The ring bend, steps 3 & 4. (*J. Shaw*)

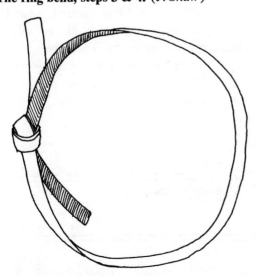

The ring bend, step 5. (*J. Shaw*)

knot, as indeed with all knots, it is essential that several inches of end should protrude from the knot.

Prusik Knot   This knot has the very useful attribute that it slides easily on another rope when slack, but jams securely when weight is put on it. It is formed with a sling passed around a single rope of greater thickness. The friction of the sling on the rope can be increased by making additional wraps.

The prusik is used, primarily, where the climber has to ascend a hanging rope. Its use is essential in crevasse rescue, and most climbers move on heavily crevassed glaciers with the loops already tied onto the rope. The prusik slings must be of a thinner diameter than the main rope and, preferably, of a softer nylon. In order to ascend a hanging rope, two, or better still, three prusik loops should be attached to it. Two loops are for the feet and the third passes round the climber's chest to

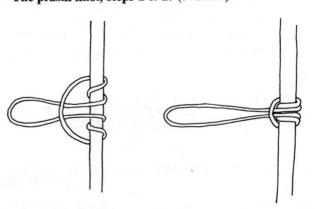

The prusik knot, steps 1 & 2. (*J. Shaw*)

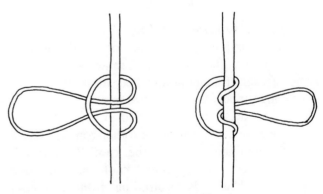

The prusik knot, steps 3 & 4. (*J. Shaw*)

maintain balance. One of the foot loops is slid up the rope, while the climber's weight is taken on the other. The climber then stands up in the higher loop and his weight jams the knot. The chest prusik is slid up the rope as high as possible, then the process is repeated for the other foot. The technique needs considerable practice and the prusik loops must be of the correct length. If it is envisaged that the climber will spend much time ascending fixed ropes on a climb, a prusiking device, such as a jumar clamp, is usually carried. This device, which works in a similar way, moving freely except under load, is much faster in use than the prusik.

Another use for the prusik loop, as mentioned before, is during a steep rappel. If the rappel to be embarked on is unknown, or ends in an overhanging situation, a prusik loop should be fixed to the rope before the descent and attached to the climber. The loop can then be slid down the rope as the climber rappels. If the rappel gets out of control, the knot will jam and hold the climber.

The Fisherman's Knot This is the best knot for joining two ropes of equal thickness together. This situation often arises during the descent of a mountain when, in order to make long rappels, two ropes are joined.

An overhand knot is tied in the end of one rope, and the end of the other rope is passed through the center of the knot. That end is then tied in an overhand knot round the first rope. The ends protruding from the knot should point in opposite directions and lie parallel to the ropes.

In order to make a long rappel, two ropes of equal length are often tied together with a fisherman's knot. A sling is placed over a projection on the rock or around a chockstone. The rope is passed through the sling and hung down the rock with both ends of equal length. You must always make sure that the rope that has the knot in it *below* the sling is pulled, so that the knot does not have to pass through the sling, where it might jam.

Coiling the Rope The simplest method of making the rope into a coil is to form it into loops, each one of which is the length of your outstretched arms. The resulting diameter of the coil is about two feet. When about three feet is remaining at the end of the rope, bend the starting end into a bight, wind the three-foot end around and around the coil tightly, working toward the bight, and pass the end through the bight. The bight is then pulled to trap the end.

This is a quick method, but the coil formed is difficult to carry. It tends to get in the way if the descent is steep and often slips from the shoulder. A better method for long or steep carries is the backpack coil. In this coil, the rope is doubled. Two arms' lengths of the ends of the rope are used to tie off the coil and form the straps to carry it over your back. The remaining doubled rope is laid in loops, either side of an upturned palm. When the rope has been gathered in this way, the free ends are wound three times around, near the head of the coil, and a hitch is formed through the resulting bight. Then the coil can be hung on the back with a single end going over each shoulder, crossing over the coil at the back, and being secured around the waist at the front.

The fisherman's knot, steps 1 & 2. (*J. Shaw*)

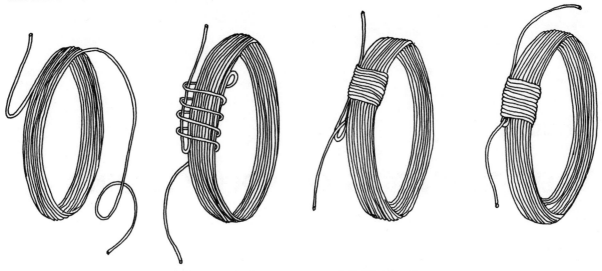

The rope coil, steps 1, 2, 3 & 4. (*J. Shaw*)

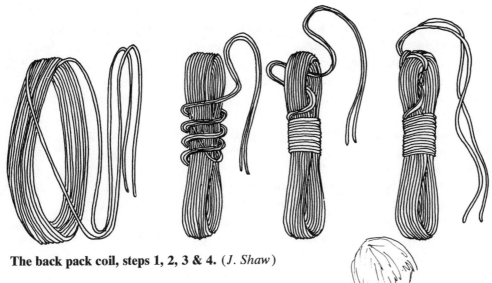

The back pack coil, steps 1, 2, 3 & 4. (*J. Shaw*)

The consequences of a wrongly tied knot can be so serious that great care must be taken to tie knots correctly. Practice these knots before your first climb until they can be tied accurately and quickly. If in doubt, consult someone who is experienced and, once you are confident in your knot-tying ability, always cast your eye over knots tied by beginners with whom you are climbing.

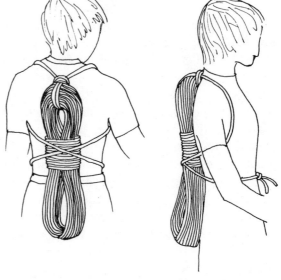

The back pack coil, steps 5 & 6. (*J. Shaw*)

Chapter 7

BASIC TECHNIQUES OF ROCK CLIMBING

Any instruction in the art of climbing must begin with the feet. Imagine a ladder placed at an incline against a wall. To climb it you step up from rung to rung using your hands for balance. Hardly any weight is taken on your hands and arms. If you did climb the ladder using mainly your arm strength you would be exhausted even after a short distance. The same is true in climbing.

There are situations where arm strength is important, but even on steep rock, the feet are more important. Once, priding myself on the ability to do about forty pullups, I had to admit defeat on an overhanging pitch and let a friend, who could only chin himself to a bar three times, lead it. I had tried to pull myself up the climb mainly using handholds, whereas he had carefully selected his footholds, using his hands for balance and conserving his strength. So the placement of the feet is paramount.

Back to the ladder. If you try to climb it while leaning in, you will find it difficult. First, you won't be able to see where you are putting your feet; second, you will have to use much more effort to climb it; and third, the angle of your body will be constantly trying to push your feet off the rungs. The way to climb a ladder, then, is to keep a vertical position using your hands for balance. When you get to rock you will find the same principle applies.

Practice first on a low-angled slab, perhaps at a local disused quarry or on the bank of a river or lake. Find one that is not too high and move around on it. When you are close to the ground allow your body to hug the slab and you will find, inevitably, that your feet will slide off from where a moment before they were perfectly balanced and secure.

The placing of feet on holds (irregularities on the rock that allow the climber to support his weight) requires some decisions. At first, like so much else in climbing, you will have to think about the problems consciously. Later, decisions will become instinctive and you will move naturally from hold to hold.

If the hold is small and sharp, like the edge of a drawer poking from a desk, put the side of your boot on it, especially if you are wearing special lightweight climbing boots. Your feet will be closer to the rock that way, and as you reach up, there will be less of a tendency for your boot to bend inward.

On a sloping, rounded hold, the secret is to keep your heel well down. In fact, whenever possible, the angle of the sole of your boot should be slightly below the horizontal while on a hold. This will tend to force your boot inward and increase the grip. Practice flexing your ankles so that you can do this comfortably while keeping the rest of your body in a vertical position. When an experienced friend gave me this advice early in my climbing career, I found that it made a considerable immediate difference in my ability. The adhesion

**Overlaps often
provide the crux of
many slab climbs.**
(*J. Shaw*)

**With the side of your boot on a hold there will
be less of a strain on your calf muscles.** (*J. Shaw*)

of your boot to the rock depends on the surface area the sole has in contact with the rock, and the angle it is to the hold.

As you move around on the slab you will gradually find that you can use smaller and smaller holds to move upward. As well as the size of holds, their position and spacing is important. One common fault of beginners is to try to step too high onto a hold. It's much better to use small intermediate holds than to make a giant step upward. As you lift one foot a great distance, you will find that it is almost impossible to prevent the heel of the foot that is on the hold from lifting. And when the heel lifts, the toe begins to be pushed backward off the hold. So, look around carefully and get into the habit of using the smaller holds. You will find that you will be climbing more gracefully and with greater security.

A good climber should move like a cat. Imagine that you are trying to creep up the rock with as little noise and sudden movement as possible. If you do this, then you will become accustomed to doing the right things. To move quietly you have to select the hold you are going to use, carefully. Then you will gently move your boot onto it, placing it on the hold in the correct position the first time. There will be no noise, no commotion, no fuss.

The next essential step of good movement is to get your body over the hold. This sounds elementary, but many people have to consciously put their bodies in this position. Place your foot on the hold, then move your body sideways until your weight is pressing down on the hold. Straighten your leg smoothly, gradually applying the force. Continue the movement until the leg is fully locked. If you need any convincing that this is important, try standing on even a partially bent leg for any length of time.

Resist the temptation to move your foot around on the hold; get it right the first time. Make sure that your foot is still firmly on the hold, then begin to move your other foot. Generally, you should not move more than one of your points of contact with the rock at any one time. This gives a considerable margin of safety, since if one of the holds should break or your hand or foot should slip, you will be able to maintain your balance. If the slab you have found is suitable, experiment with the placing of your foot in cracks. Often you will find you can jam the toe of the boot into the crack just above a narrowing. Then, when your weight comes over it, the boot will be securely held. Cracks offer the best footholds. Often the trouble is disengaging the foot after you have moved up! If the crack is of a width greater than your boot, it may offer a hold on either of its walls or you may be able to fix your boot across it, either horizontally, or if the crack is narrower, at an angle.

As you climb around try descending and traversing as well. Beginners often find descending difficult. Here it is even more important to keep your body well away from the rock so you can see the holds. If the angle is fairly easy, then you should face out—but resist the temptation to sit down. When the angle steepens, a sideways descent is preferred, and only when the rock becomes very steep, should you face in toward it. Though you can get secure handholds in this position, it is sometimes difficult to place your feet correctly on the holds.

Descent is of equal importance to ascent, and from the first, you should get used to climbing down difficult rock. This will increase your confidence immensely. Later, when leading difficult climbs, you'll often find yourself in a situation where, having climbed up to the difficult section of the pitch, you'll have to descend to take a rest or to think over the moves. If you have not been in the habit of climbing down, such a situation is no time to learn because you'll generally be a little tired and often "gripped." Also, when you begin to climb mountains it will be important for safety reasons that you can descend quickly and safely, often on an unknown route.

So far we have considered the use of the feet. The use of the hands comes much more naturally, at least when gripping an edge of

In descent, it is often better to turn sideways. (*J. Shaw*)

rock. Try not to grip too tightly; tense muscles tire out fast. Use as much of your hand as possible; even your little finger's pressure on a hold can improve your grip. Keep your hands between about the top of your head and your waist level. If you stretch too far with your hands, your body will be pulled out of balance and you will not be able to see where your feet are going. Of course you will often meet the situation where the only hold you can use is one that is at the limit of your reach, but before using it, you should carefully check that you are not neglecting some smaller, closer hold.

HANDHOLDS

Holds come in all shapes, sizes, and positions. What is important is that the combination of hand- and footholds you choose should feel right and not interfere with your balance.

The easiest of all holds to use is the large incut hold where your fingers can curl over and behind it. It is often called a jug handle, and the hand fits naturally round it, giving a great feeling of security.

When the hold is smaller it is referred to as a fingerhold. Here you should try to keep the rest of your hand as close as possible to the rock, with the first and second joints of your finger pointing downward toward the hold. This position will tend to prevent your fingers being levered off the hold.

Often you will have to employ side holds as you move up. Your hands are used in opposition to each other or to your foot. A considerable force can be exerted this way. Try lifting a suitcase by pressing your hands on its sides. Of course, moving up in this situation means that you are using strength in your fingers, and you have to obtain a secure foothold before you release the pressure.

Another similar hold is the pinch grip where the opposing forces keeping your fingers on the rock are exerted by your fingers and thumb. Again this can be a surprisingly secure hold.

Good holds can also be found under the lip

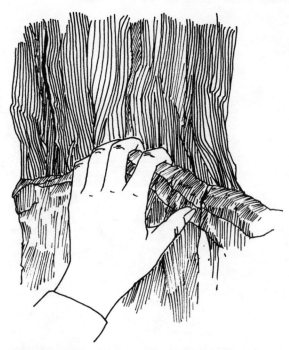

A fine handhold. Even a steep climb can be easy with holds like this, using as much of your hand as possible. (*J. Shaw*)

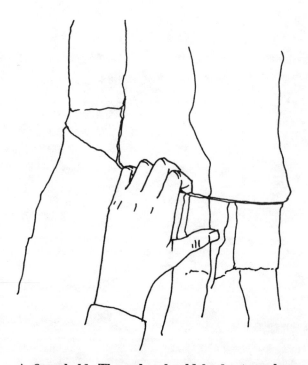

A fingerhold. The palm should be kept as close as possible to the rock to minimize leverage on the fingertips. Note that the grip is by the fingertips rather than with the entire hand as with the handhold. (*J. Shaw*)

On a slab the hands are kept low and the movements are delicate and unhurried. The Apron in Yosemite has many fine slab routes. (*J. Shaw*)

A pinch hold on the flake helps the climber to lean out and find a finger jam in the crack. (*R. Shaw*)

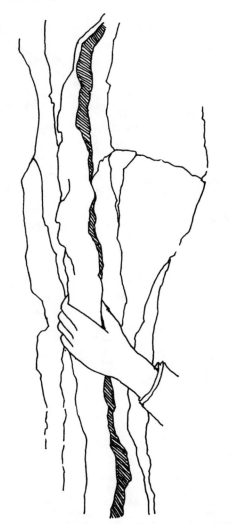

Once you get used to pinch holds you will find them frequently and be surprised at the security they offer. (*J. Shaw*)

of a projecting section of rock. This type of hold, called an undercling, needs to be used in opposition to pressure on the footholds. With this hold, as with others, the farther you can lean back, the less adequate the foothold needs to be. With a good handhold on an otherwise smooth face of rock you can, by leaning out, walk your feet up. The opposition of forces is the secret of much good climbing technique, and the next chapter will deal with its use in specialized situations.

An important habit to acquire right at the beginning is that of rhythm. Try to climb smoothly, combining a series of moves rather than taking each move individually. When you move you acquire momentum, and the more flowing your ascent, the more you utilize the momentum to carry you. At first you will find it difficult. You will probably have to treat each move separately. But as soon as possible, try to think of moves in combination. This enables you to move quickly over a difficult stretch from resting place to resting place. Gradually, you will be able to look at a stretch of rock and say, "If I put my left foot there and get a side pull on that edge, then I can move my right foot to that small incut hold; and with my right hand in the crack, I can get my left foot on the sloping hold and my right will go onto the ledge." Once you have worked it out, you can make the movements one after the other without pausing. This ability is essential when you tackle an overhang, since to spend much time out of balance is to risk falling off through exhaustion.

Climbers often liken their sport to chess. In any given situation there are usually several combinations of moves possible, though one solution may be more elegant than the others. The ability to think ahead and recognize the options open is an invaluable aid to the climber and one of the great pleasures of the sport. A good climb is satisfying to the mind, as well as the body.

Having gained some experience of moving on a reasonably angled slab, the time has come to find a companion and put on the rope.

If you can find someone who has climbed before to lead you, so much the better. If not, then you need to exercise additional care. Choose an area where others climb and seek their advice as to the best route to begin on. You will be looking for one that is not too steep, is plentifully supplied with good sound holds, and is short, say about fifty to a hundred feet. At this height someone could drop the end of a rope to you from above, if you got into difficulties. If you can find a route that allows an easy escape if you fail to get up a pitch, so much the better. If a guidebook ex-

The opposing forces of the feet hold the climber on the steep rock despite poor handholds. (*R. Shaw*)

Leaning back on a good edge, the climber can make use of steeply sloping footholds. (*R. Shaw*)

The classic position on a slab. Hands low, heels low, and body erect. (*R. Shaw*)

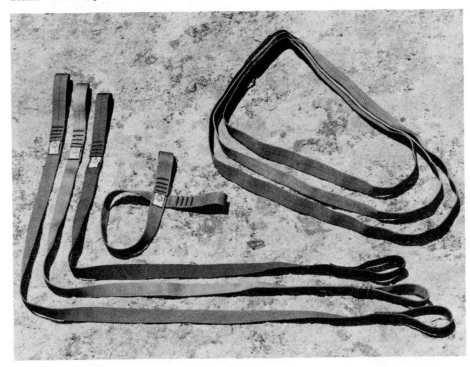

Slings of different lengths for belaying. Sewn slings such as these reduce the runner's bulk. They are made from one-inch tubular nylon. Those with a loop at either end are ideal for threading through tunnels or behind the flakes. (*D. Hall. Courtesy, Forrest Mountaineering*)

ists for the cliff, buy it. In it you will find careful descriptions of the known climbs and their standard of difficulty. The grading of climbs varies from area to area, but the guidebook will usually indicate how its grading system compares with others, and it will always be obvious which are the easier climbs. The store where you bought your equipment will be able to help you and may put you in touch with a climbing club or an individual prepared to start you off.

If you can't find anyone experienced, don't be discouraged. Many climbers have started the sport without the benefit of assistance from a more-experienced climber, or even from a book. Just exercise your common sense, err on the side of safety, and never let false pride be your motivation.

STAGING A FIRST CLIMB

So here you are at the bottom of the cliff, your companion and you tied on to the ends of a 150-foot nylon rope using one of the knots described in Chapter 6. You are going to lead the first pitch. You look at it carefully. It runs up a series of obvious holds to a ledge far above. It is not too steep and there are intermediate ledges where you can relax. Around your neck you hang a selection of nylon tape slings and carabiners and, either from your harness, or from a bandolier, a rack of nuts on wire loops. Do not burden yourself too much.

Your partner finds a suitable belay near the start. It may be a tree he can tie himself to, or he may find a stone jammed in the crack to loop a sling around. Once the sling is looped around the tree or the jammed stone, your partner should tie a double figure-eight knot in his end of the rope and clip it to the sling with a carabiner. Now he cannot be dislodged, which is important even at the bottom of a climb since if you fell off, having placed a runner, your companion would be jerked upward.

Once the belay is secure you can begin your climb. Try to achieve an even-paced rhythm as you climb, but resist the temptation to move too fast. If you have chosen wisely, the

The leader, though on a small ledge, is belayed securely to a good spike and is ready to bring the second up. (*R. Shaw*)

climbing will probably seem very easy. Treat it seriously however, and concentrate on climbing gracefully.

After, say, ten feet, you should place some protection to avoid a fall to the ground should you slip, though you may not feel the need for it as yet. Look around at the natural features of the rock and see what you can make of them. There may be a spike over which you can drop a tape sling, or you may have to select one of your nuts to jam in a crack. Look for a position where a crack narrows. The nut will slide in above the bottleneck and jam there with any downward pressure. Test your protection by giving it a firm downward pull, and once you are satisfied with it, fix a carabiner onto the sling or wire loop, and click your rope through it. Before you do this, look ahead and see which direction you will be moving in. Make sure that the rope will run easily through the carabiner when you climb on.

Once you have fixed this running belay, you are much safer than you were a minute before. Now if you fall off, your friend with the rope around his waist will be able to stop your falling all the way to the ground. If you are three feet above the running belay, you will fall six feet before the rope comes tight.

You continue up the climb, fixing other runners as the opportunity presents itself. With each running belay fixed the friction on the rope increases, and if you have placed too many, you may find that the rope behind you will hardly move.

If you are climbing in a straight line, a large number of runners may be placed without too much drag on the rope, since the rope will run easily through the carabiners without friction-creating bends. If, on the other hand, the route zigzags up the face, great care must be exercised not to put so much friction on the rope, otherwise you may find yourself unable to move. The problem can be partially overcome on a meandering route by lengthening the sling to achieve as near to a straight rope behind you as possible.

Now you have reached the ledge and are going to bring your friend up to join you. When you are safely on the ledge and have found a suitable anchor by attaching yourself to a sling and carabiner placed round a spike or a chockstone (where possible it is best to have more than one anchor) you shout down "Off Belay" to tell the belayer that you are secure and do not need the safety of the belay rope any longer. The reply to this is "Belay Off," and the belayer can now begin to remove his anchor and get ready to follow you. You are securely fixed on the ledge to one or more slings. Your responsibility is a great one. The anchor must be a sound one so that if your friend slips, you can withstand any jerk without being dislodged. Once you are belayed you should stand or sit with the rope taut between you and the anchor. Then if your companion does slip, the pull on the belay will be a steady one and not a snatch.

When you are sure that everything is sound, you put the rope around your waist and call down "On Belay" and then, once you have taken in the rope, "Climb."

As your friend climbs you take the rope in steadily, by feeding it from one hand around the back of your waist to the other hand, feeling him on the end of it, like a fish on a line. Neither hand should be taken off the rope, but one hand should be slid along it, while the other holds it fast. The friction of the rope running around the waist is an essential element of the system. You must not pull too tight otherwise you may dislodge him from his holds, or at least, spoil his enjoyment. If you do pull too tight or if the climber needs to step down a few moves he will call "Slack." If, on the other hand, you have not been taking in the rope as the climber ascends, the call will come "Up Rope." It is very important that no slack develops in the climbing rope, otherwise, if the climber falls, it may be for a long way and the jerk on the belayer will be considerable, possibly causing injury to both.

Eventually, your partner joins you on the ledge. If he is going to lead the next pitch, there is little rearrangement necessary. You can remain secured to your belay, noting that

In a situation like this the second appreciates a leader who takes in the rope
steadily. The West Buttress of the Bastille, Eldorado Canyon, Boulder, Colorado.
(*R. Shaw*)

it is capable of taking both an upward and a downward pull, and your friend climbs on, placing running belays as before. If, however, you are going to do the leading, you have to change belays.

This is a dangerous moment, especially if you are on a very small ledge with only one anchor. You must be methodical. Still holding your partner on the rope round your waist, tie a figure-eight knot in it about five feet from your partner's waist and clip it into the carabiner to which you are belayed. You are now both safe, and once your companion has settled down and placed your rope round his waist, you can unclip your belay from the carabiner, leaving his still clipped in, and proceed to climb.

It is important to ensure that both of you are never off belay at the same time. Once, on a steep and difficult climb, a friend who had just led the pitch brought me up to a good grass ledge. When I arrived on it, he began to remove his belay. Just at that moment, the grass ledge disappeared from under us and we were left grasping at the rock, with disaster imminent if either of us slipped. Luckily, neither of us did, and we consequently learned this good lesson.

If your friend has climbed on, rather than changing belays with you, you pay out the rope smoothly, and unless you are using a belaying device, which is fully discussed in Chapter 8, you should be wearing gloves. Arresting the slide of a nylon rope around your waist creates a lot of heat, and unprotected hands suffer severe rope burns. Moreover, it may prove impossible to stop a long leader fall without the protection of gloves.

Watch carefully as your friend climbs. There is no worse feeling than to lead a difficult section of rock and look down to see the second gazing off at the superb view. It makes you feel very lonely. And the situation is dangerous. If the second is not paying attention, he may not feed the rope out when the leader moves up. It is not a pleasant sensation to step up on a small hold while the rope jerks behind you. So pay attention to how you manage the rope, letting it out as the leader climbs and retrieving it if he retreats. If there is a fall, you may be able to pull in some of the slack before the rope goes taut and prevent a longer fall.

The leader may well disappear from your view before he completes the pitch. Then you will not know what is happening except by the way the rope moves. Eventually you will hear the call "Off Belay" and you can reply "Belay Off" and get yourself ready to follow. Brief and precise calls are very important, and you should practice them until they become automatic. Once, when I was leading a friend up a fairly difficult climb on a windy day, I heard his shout of "Slack" above the wind and fed him a foot or so of rope. Again the call came, this time sounding rather frantic. I payed out another foot or so of rope. Then, with a tremendous jerk that almost winded me and dragged me hard onto the belay, the rope came tight. When my friend eventually reached the belay ledge in a rather flustered condition, I discovered he had been shouting "Take in the Slack!" rather than the correct call of "Up Rope." I, of course, had only heard the last word of his urgent call.

Once the climber above is secured, he will call down "On Belay" and take in the rope until it is taut. At this point, and not earlier, you should remove your belay. Then, when he has called "Climb," you begin to move up toward him. Do not move too quickly; the belayer will have difficulty taking the rope in fast enough. Climb steadily, enjoy yourself, and take the opportunity of being second on the rope to practice different ways of placing your hands and feet.

Now, back to your original slab to learn another technique that is a vital one in mountaineering and is great fun. This is the technique called the rappel. Imagine that you have climbed to a ledge on a face and can go no farther. If the rock below you is not too difficult, you can climb down. However, if it is too steep or the route is unknown to you, it can be descended on a double rope by a rappel.

The principle behind this technique is that the friction of the rope around the climber's

Classic rappel. Make sure the rope is kept off the neck or a nasty rope burn may result. (*J. Shaw*)

body, or on a special device, makes a controlled descent possible. If you are careful and methodical, the method is a very safe one; if not, it can be dangerous. Many good climbers have been killed while rappelling, usually through carelessness. There are a variety of methods, but they all depend on a suitable strong anchor, such as a spike of rock or a strongly wedged chockstone. If the anchor is doubtful, do not use it. Or, if you must, say,

in the descent of a mountain when no other way is possible, test it thoroughly while protected by a safety rope from another belay. When you are satisfied with the anchor, arrange a sling over it and pass the rope through the sling. Tie the ends of the rope together and equalize the rope on both sides of the sling. Now throw the rope clear of the cliff so that it hangs directly down from the anchor. Once the rappel has been completed the rope can be pulled down, running through the sling which is abandoned, and the process repeated until the base of the mountain is reached.

The first method to learn is the classic method. This is hardly ever used now, but it has the great advantage in that it depends on no other equipment. If you find yourself in an emergency on a mountain when you have lost your rappelling device and carabiners, then you can still descend safely using this method.

Stand astride the doubled rope, pick it up behind you and bring it across your right hip, over your left shoulder, and into your right hand. You are now ready to descend. With your left hand (the position is reversed if you are left-handed) on the rope above you, and your right hand holding the rope that hangs below, you simply lean back and walk down the cliff. You will find that the friction of the rope round your body supports your weight and you will hardly have to grip the rope at all. Your right hand is the most important one; after you have walked a few steps, take your left hand off the rope and you will find that you have only been using it for balance.

The friction with this type of rappel is so great that you will have to feed the rope with your right hand; your body weight alone will hardly move it. This makes it a very safe method of rappelling but an uncomfortable one. It is essential that you wear a stout parka as the heat generated by the friction can produce a burn on your shoulder if you are careless.

An improved version of this rappel involves the use of a sling and carabiner as a cradle. Twist a sling into a figure eight and put a leg through each loop. Then clip a carabiner into

The sling rappel. More comfortable by far. Notice the angle of the body to the rock and the way the body is turned partly to one side. (*J. Shaw*)

the sling. Now, instead of passing the doubled rope between your legs, you clip it through the carabiner, and pass the rope across your chest, over your left shoulder and into your right hand as before. When you try this rappel you will find that the friction is much less and the descent is smoother and more comfort-

able. A long rappel, especially if sections of it are overhanging and the climber swings in space, can generate a lot of heat.

Hence, the popularity of devices that take away the need for the rope to pass around the climber's body: One method that needs only carabiners is to pass the rope through interlocked carabiners. The chain of carabiners is fixed to a sling around the climber's legs or to the climbing harness.

The brake bar is another device that substitutes a metal bar that lies across the carabiner. This small device is easy to operate but can put a dangerous strain on the gate of the carabiner. Also the heat created by the friction of the rope over the bar is not easily dissipated and may make the bar so hot that it damages the rope, especially if the climber stops after a long, fast descent.

Another device is the figure-eight descender. Once in position it is foolproof, but it has several disadvantages. It kinks the rope rather badly and this can lead to the rope jamming on the anchor sling when the time comes to retrieve it. Moreover, the figure eight has to be removed from your cradle before the rope can be passed through it and can easily be dropped, especially if you are fumbling with gloved hands in a storm. A similar device, called the Longhorn, produced by Mountain Safety Research, appears to have solved these problems, and has the added advantage that the rope can be locked round it if the climber wants to stop his descent.

Some of the devices used for rappelling can also be used to belay with. Instead of the belayer passing the rope round his waist, he pays it out through one of these devices attached to his climbing harness. Then, if the leader falls, the belay device absorbs much of the strain that usually would be on the belayer's hands. One of the best belaying aids is the Sticht Plate. It is very simple to operate and very effective, though it does require practice to feed the rope smoothly.

In general, it is only worthwhile acquiring a rappelling device if you intend to use it also for belaying, or if you are tackling mountains

A rappel from Cathedral Peak in the Sierras. To increase the friction on the steep rappel, the climber has passed the rope around her thigh. It is safer to use locking carabiners with this rappel. (*R. Shaw*)

The angle of the body is too close to the horizontal here, making the descent more tiring than it need be and rather precarious. (*R. Shaw*)

A free rappel is a rappel where for most of the descent the climber does not come into contact with the rock. The climber here is using a rappel device that takes much of the strain out of a free rappel. (*R. Shaw*)

where you are likely to need to make long descents by rappel. Otherwise it is one more piece of equipment to add to your burden.

SOME TIPS WHEN RAPPELLING

Always carry a rope sling or two with you. Once on the descent from an overhanging cliff, my parka jammed the rope in the carabiner I was using to rappel on. Luckily, I had with me a rope sling which I was able to fix on the rope using a prusik knot. Then I could put my foot in the loop of the sling, stand up and take the weight off the carabiner. There are a variety of situations when it is important to be able to take the strain off your rappel cradle, and even to reascend the rope. Prusik slings will enable you to do this. How to tie and use them is illustrated in Chapter 6.

Always tie the ends of the rope together. Should you lose your grip on the rope as you rappel, a knot in the end will prevent your sliding off into space. Also, you may find when you reach the end of the rope that you are hanging free from the rock. In this situation you may have to hang and consider what to do. A large knot in the end of the rope will enable you to do this in safety.

The first climber down should check that the rope will slide freely around the anchor sling, before the second climber starts the descent. On too many occasions I've started to pull the rope down and had it jam, either through severe twists in the rope or a bad anchor placement. Then there's no alternative but to reclimb to the anchor, if it is possible, or abandon the rope. Never, in any circumstances, try to climb back up the rope, since it may suddenly loosen as you climb causing a dangerous fall.

When you are descending a rappel, do it smoothly. In a practice situation with the rope attached to a fail-safe belay, it is great sport to leap down the face. But anyone who does this in a real rappelling situation on a mountain or cliff is courting disaster. A smooth descent puts as little strain on the anchor as possible and enables you to control your landing.

Use carabiners with a screwgate. When the rope is twisting around a carabiner or when a rappelling device is fixed to a carabiner, it may click open. With a screwgate carabiner this danger is removed.

Be very cautious about using anchor slings left by previous parties. Nylon tape or rope is damaged by the heat created when another rope is drawn over it. Ultraviolet light also weakens nylon. So, if the sling does not appear to be in very good condition, do not use it, but substitute one of your own. On popular descent routes you may find that the anchor slings are threaded through a metal link. Pass your rope through this link. The rope will run much more easily when you retrieve it and there will be no damage to the anchor sling.

The rappel then, is a very important technique in the mountaineer's repertoire. It is enjoyable, fast, and, with proper caution, safe. Complete concentration is demanded when setting up the rappel. You should always practice rappel methods in a safe place and use a safety rope. Even once you have mastered the techniques, use a safety rope wherever possible or fix a prusik loop from your harness to the rope above the carabiner or rappel device.

Chapter 8

BELAYING FOR PROTECTION

The essence of safety in climbing is the belay. Without adequate belays the lives of the whole party are put in jeopardy not just the life of the leader. When the belay is to be used to secure the second climber while he safeguards the leader, or for a rappel anchor, it must be totally safe. The failure of a belay in these circumstances will result in a severe accident. Consequently, the greatest care should be exercised in selecting and fixing these belays. Wherever possible they should be made up of more than one anchor and, in the case of the second's belay, should be capable of taking a strong pull in any direction. In the case of running belays, the strength is not so crucial, though obviously the best placement will be sought. A weak running belay can absorb some of the energy of the fall, even if it breaks.

Belays can be made in four different ways using natural features, metal chocks, pitons, and bolts.

Natural Features. These should be the first choice of the climber. Their use involves the minimum of environmental damage and they provide the soundest of belays. Often they can be used in conjunction with a chock. A sling can be placed over a spike that will take a downward pull, and a chock can be inserted in a crack to restrain an upward load. If the natural feature is a large one, such as a small pinnacle, the climbing rope itself can be used

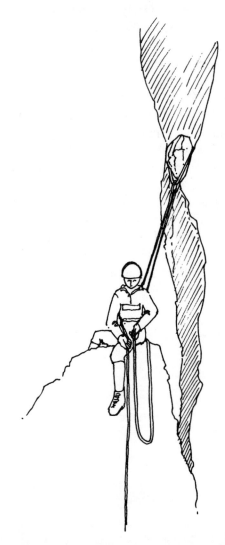

A secure natural belay around a chockstone. If possible, it is always safer to sit when belaying. (*J. Shaw*)

to form the fixed belay. Here the rope is placed over the pinnacle or block and a bight is tied off in a figure eight and clipped into a carabiner on the climber's harness. Similarly, a bight of the rope can be threaded behind a large natural chockstone and tied off in the same way.

Metal Chocks. Until fairly recently the only means of belaying open to climbers was through natural features or pitons or bolts hammered into the rock. Developments in Britain in the use of stones inserted in cracks and jammed knotted slings, then machine bolts, and finally custom-made chocks have changed that. A very wide selection of metal chocks is now available for the climber to use in a multitude of situations. The chock, on a wire or tape loop, is jammed into a crack and the belay is made to it using a carabiner. With ingenuity and a large enough rack of chocks, protection can be found from almost any crack. Unlike the piton or the bolt, the chock does little if any damage and does not mark the route for future climbers. Usually the chock is placed in the crack just above a narrowing and worked downward with the hand until it jams. In poor cracks several chocks can be combined to form an effective anchor either by using them in opposition or by stacking them. When using chocks in opposition, it is useful to use a sliding half hitch on the carabiners to adjust the tension and to equalize the load on each chock. When the crack is too wide to secure the available chock, another chock may be jammed alongside it in a stack to effect jamming. Tapered chocks are best for this, though with ingenuity and patience any combination of chocks may jam securely.

Thought has to be given not only to the strength of a particular chock placement, but to whether it will come off as the rope runs through it. It is a circumstance calculated to concentrate the mind wonderfully if, when you are struggling on the crux of a pitch, you hear the tinkling sound of your runner sliding down the rope. To prevent this, the first

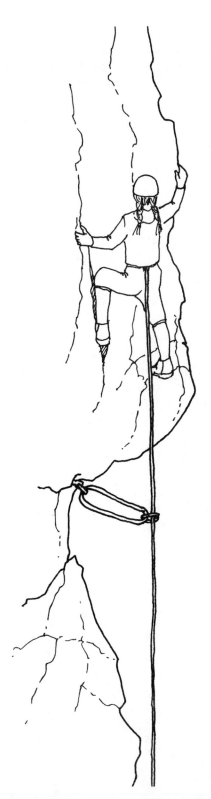

The climber, having correctly placed a sling runner below the bulge, is using the opposing pressure of the hands on the edge and a crack to maintain balance. (*J. Shaw*)

course of action is to ensure, where possible, that the carabiners attached to each chock let the rope run in as straight a line as possible. You can do this by attaching an additional sling to the chock sling. The other possibility is to fix another chock whose only purpose is to keep the runner chock in position.

When the time comes to remove a chock, force is the least useful action. Think first; examine the crack and decide where the chock has to be moved to before you touch it. Many climbers carry a long bladelike hooked tool to facilitate the removal of chocks, but gentleness and patience are probably the best tools.

Pitons. Before the introduction of chocks these were in wide use but, except on new ascents, on serious mountains, or in winter when cracks are likely to be filled with ice, their use is in decline. Climbers have long been disturbed by the damage done to the rock by their use, especially in popular areas. Cracks have widened considerably on some often-climbed routes in areas like Yosemite, and the rock is scarred by hammer blows. Now, to see a climber carrying them is unusual, and even long routes that were once only possible by hammering pitons into cracks are done using chocks.

An illustration of a piton runner that would cause great problems for the leader above the bulge. (*J. Shaw*)

A strongly constructed piton hammer. (*D. Van Pelt. Courtesy, Forrest Mountaineering*)

Mountaineering is a game with no fixed rules; each climber must decide what ethics to adhere to. My position is that pitons have no place on any route that has been done without their assistance, and on new routes only if the climber is an expert who judges that the route is impossible without their use. In many areas pitons exist on routes, left there by previous climbers for protection or aid. The existing protection pitons in a long-established route

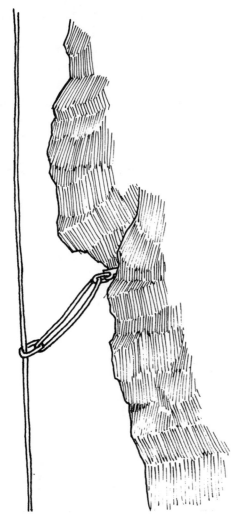

The correct way to use such a runner placement. A sling has been clipped to the piton to allow the rope to hang clear of the rock. (*J. Shaw*)

Bolts. What has been said about pitons applies with even greater force to the question of bolts. Bolting changes the rock forever, unlike pitons which are hammered into natural cracks. Moreover, with the use of enough bolts any piece of rock can be climbed and the standard of the climb may not be very high. Only the climber of the very highest ability should use bolts and then only in a situation where their use is essential. However, bearing in mind that what was essential yesterday may be optional tomorrow, the placing of bolts is a very serious action since a piece of rock, which might at a future date be climbed by more natural means, has been permanently disfigured. Though I have placed a bolt for a belay on a new route, in retrospect I think I was wrong. There are areas, however, like the Apron in Yosemite, where climbs are only justifiable through the use of bolts for protection.

A bolt used as a belay on a smooth slab. Without such a belay any ascent would be extremely dangerous. (*P. Ross*)

should be left in place. This prevents damage to the rock caused by their removal and subsequent replacement. With aid pitons I feel it is legitimate in most cases to remove them if the climber who does so can, without their aid, lead the pitch. However, there are certain situations when the pitons are best left in place, as for example, on a long route of a reasonable standard with a short aid section that would become an extremely difficult climb if one or two pitons were removed. In the last analysis, each climber must decide; mountaineering has no Supreme Court.

The Placing of Runners. A little has already been said about the ways in which runners can be constructed. Several principles have been touched on: The runners should remain in place; they should, as far as possible, allow the rope to run in a straight line from the belayer; and they should be arranged to add the minimum of drag to the rope, usually by altering the length of the sling, as for example, under an overhang. It also must be empha-

sized that the runner can protect or endanger the second climber, and the leader must remember to make allowance for this. Consider, for example, the situation where a leader climbs a crack to an overhang then traverses twenty feet right to another crack which he ascends to a ledge. If too many runners are put on in the first crack the drag on the rope will be severe by the time the leader gets up the second crack, especially if he has put pro-

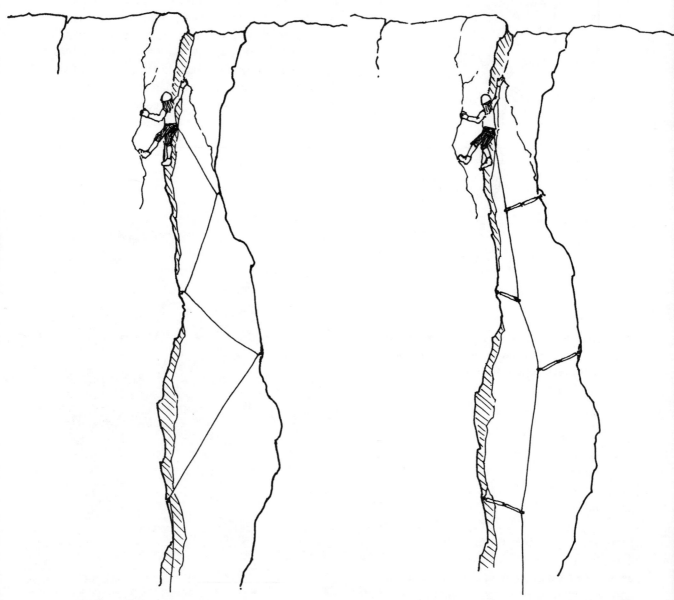

Careless placing of runners can make rope drag excessive. (*J. Shaw*)

The correct use of slings to minimize rope drag when the placements are not in a straight line. (*J. Shaw*)

Stemming out of a deep crack. A classic case of bad runner placement. The drag on the climber has already become excessive. A long sling runner was needed here to keep the rope out of the crack. (*S. Hilbert. Courtesy, Idaho State University, Outdoor Program*)

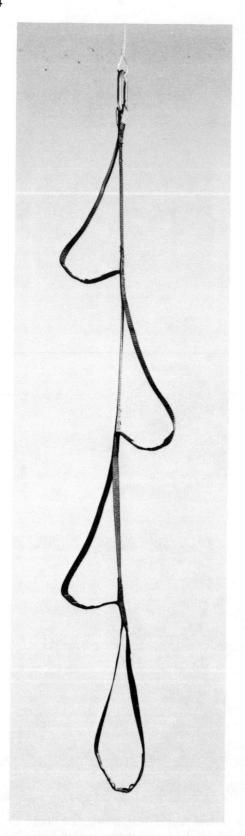

A modern tape étrier used in aid climbing.
(*D. Hall. Courtesy, Forrest Mountaineering*)

tection in that too. However, a good runner at the top of the first crack will protect the second as he climbs. Conversely, a runner at the bottom of the second crack will endanger him, as the rope will run horizontally during his traverse. If protection is not placed until near the top of the second crack, the rope will be at an angle to the second and at worst he will suffer a pendulum.

Traversing creates the greatest problems for the second, unless he is as competent as the leader. On an especially difficult section, the traverse can be safeguarded by the second leaving the runner and allowing his rope to remain clipped to it. The rope is then run through another carabiner on the second's harness and he moves across until the stance is reached. Then the second unties and the rope is pulled through the runner and back to the stance. Of course, in this situation the runner is lost.

On some steep pitches, the second may get into difficulties and fall off. If the climb is very steep, the second may find himself hanging in space, clear of the rock. In this situation, if the leader cannot lower him to a resting place, the use of prusik loops may be the only answer. The prusik knot, which is illustrated in Chapter 6, will slide on a rope when slack, but jam when a load is put on it. With two loops for the feet, and preferably a chest loop, the climber can ascend the rope.

Direct Aid. When a stretch of rock, or even an entire face, cannot be climbed using only the natural features, the climber has to resort to direct aid. In this, progress is achieved by using pitons hammered into cracks or jammed chocks and étrier or stirrups usually made of tape webbing. The stirrups are hung from the piton, chock, or bolt using a carabiner, and the climber places his feet in the loops of the stirrup rather than on the rock.

It is beyond the scope of this book to deal with the specialized techniques of aid climbing. Excellent instruction in the placement and use of aid can be found in Royal Robbins' book, *Advanced Rockcraft* (see Recommended Reading).

Chapter 9

ADVANCED TECHNIQUES OF ROCK CLIMBING

Once you have progressed from the easier climbs you will need to acquire some more advanced techniques. Most of these will come naturally to you, and it will be rare when the techniques described do not have to be used in combination with each other. A crack climb may, in the space of a few feet, require the climber to bridge, jam, layback, and chimney as well as face climb on small holds.

Describing a technique in rock climbing is not the same as, for example, instructing someone how to do a snowplow in skiing or the breast stroke in swimming. Rock possesses an infinite variety. No layback is exactly like another. This chapter can only describe the elements of advanced techniques. Only experience on the rock can teach you more.

Many cracks, especially in an area like Yosemite, can be climbed only by means of a technique called **jamming.** Sometimes, a climber needs a method other than finding holds he can grip with his fingers, or on which he places his feet. For long distances the only means of ascent may be by jamming hands and feet into the crack. As confidence is gained, this is found to be a very secure way of climbing if the crack is suited to it.

In jamming the foot can be pushed into the crack toe first, and here the type of boot worn can sometimes be crucial. Where possible the boot is placed in the crack just above a narrowing. Often, in a narrow crack, this is not possible and the foot has to be turned sideways before it will go in, and the pressure has to be exerted on one of the side walls of the crack. When the crack widens, other positions of the feet become necessary: lengthwise across the crack or at an angle.

In jamming the hands we have an advantage in that the fist can be made to change shape. In a narrow crack where only the tops of the fingers can be inserted, they may be jammed by forcing them together and partially overlapping them. As the crack widens, the degree of overlap can be increased until it is possible to slip the knuckles in. At this point the hold becomes more secure, as the fingers may be bent and the opposing pressures of fingertips and knuckles will hold the hand firmly. Once the thumb can be brought inside it can be forced into the palm, and when more of the hand is inside, a fist can be made and, if necessary, twisted sideways to jam in cracks of four or five inches in width. As the crack becomes deeper and wider, more of the arm can be inserted and the elbow joint flexed until the whole of the forearm is wedged across the crack. Wider than this and the crack is developing into a narrow chimney, where it may be necessary to jam your shoulder and use your knees, or to wriggle strenuously up, holding your breath to jam your chest when you want to rest.

There is a type of crack, called an off-width

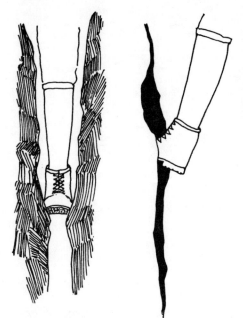

Once a secure boot jam is found, preferably just above the narrowing of the crack, the climber has the best foothold, apart from a wide ledge. (*J. Shaw*)

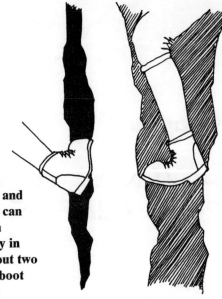

With ingenuity and experience one can jam the boot in cracks that vary in width from about two inches to your boot size. (*J. Shaw*)

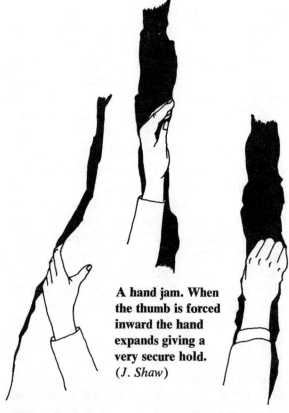

A hand jam. When the thumb is forced inward the hand expands giving a very secure hold. (*J. Shaw*)

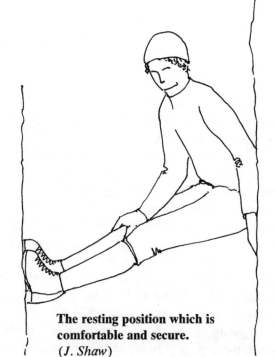

A finger jam using the tips of the fingers in a vertical crack. (*J. Shaw*)

A fist jam. The fist can be twisted to vary the pressure on the walls of the crack. (*J. Shaw*)

The resting position which is comfortable and secure. (*J. Shaw*)

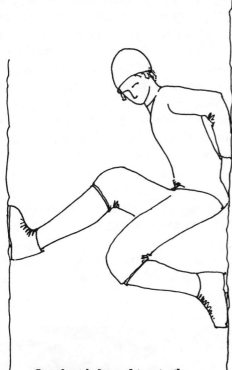

One foot is brought onto the back wall with the sole flat to the rock and the palms pressing just by the hip. (*J. Shaw*)

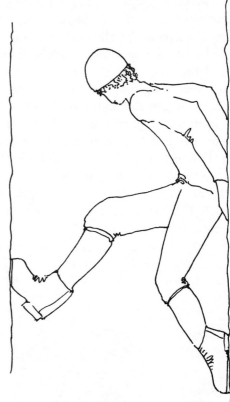

The body returns to the wall and the pressure comes off the hands and back foot. (*J. Shaw*)

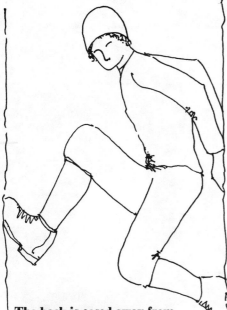

The back is eased away from the wall and the body moved upward, while the feet and the hands continue their pressure. (*J. Shaw*)

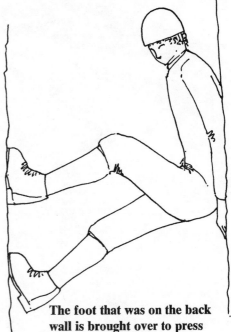

The foot that was on the back wall is brought over to press on the wall above the other foot. (*J. Shaw*)

crack, which is just too wide for jamming easily and too narrow to use the back and knees. It may sometimes be climbed by using your hands pulling in opposing directions on the walls of the crack, together with considerable ingenuity in using a variety of jamming techniques. In a good chimney the climber feels very secure. The back can be placed on one wall as the feet or knees push against the other. Upward progress is achieved usually by bringing one foot up to your seat then removing the pressure on the back and sliding it up the wall. The hands are most often below you, pressing downward on the wall.

The technique can often be a strenuous one, but practice will remove much of the effort. Moreover, it is possible to rest frequently. Though chimneys vary greatly, some general points can be made. Try to keep as far to the outside edge of the chimney as possible. This enables one to bypass any overhangs at the back of the chimney and puts one in the best position to exit onto the face when necessary. Make sure that you do not try to move up too far each time. If your back gets too far up one wall, your feet may lose their grip on the other. The same is true when raising the feet. Too high a lift and your upward progress will become strenuous and insecure. In a narrow chimney you may have to use your knees instead of your feet for upward movement.

When you are climbing a chimney do not neglect the possibility that you could **bridge** your way up it. Bridging or stemming is an el-

A steep awkward crack with few holds on the face. (*J. Shaw*)

The climber has his right foot jammed across the crack and his back against the edge of the corner. His left foot is on a friction hold on the slab. The chock runner just above him provides good security. (*Courtesy, Fantasy Ridge Mountain Guides*)

egant and efficient technique in which holds on the opposite walls of a chimney or dihedral are used, with the climber bridged across the gap. It is especially useful in corners where a bulge is encountered. In this situation the climber may surmount the overhang by bridging past it without ever being out of balance.

Dihedrals bring into play the greatest number of climbing techniques. The crack at the back of the dihedral may be jammed; either of the two faces may be climbed; progress may be made by bridging; or, it may be possible to chimney, if the dihedral is an acute one. Normally, all these techniques will come into play.

Another possibility is the use of a **layback.** This is a less common technique now that jamming techniques have developed. It calls for strength and stamina and presents the problem of changing from a semi-prone position to a vertical position. However, if the corner is right for it, it can provide a rapid and exhilarating means of ascent. The hands are placed in the corner crack, the climber leans back on them and walks his feet up the opposite wall. As the feet are walked up, the hands have to be shuffled up the crack or removed (one at a time!) and placed above each other. The problem is that the climber is held in position by the opposing forces of his arms and legs and the strain on a long steep layback is considerable. At the top of the layback a foothold or foot jam must be found to lever up onto. It is better, while laybacking, to keep the arms as straight as possible. A straight arm, like a straight leg, uses much less energy than a bent one.

Another situation that may confront the climber is that of an overhanging ledge on a steep wall, just within reach, with no holds below it and none for some way above. The type of movement to be executed here is called a **mantelshelf.** If the ledge has a good sharp incut edge and is wide, there is little problem. The climber simply grasps the edge, leans back rather as in a layback, and walks the feet up until the upper body can be moved over the ledge on straight arms. Then a foot is

On a layback the climber relies on opposing pressure of hands and feet. (*J. Shaw*)

A high step into a layback move on the Bastille Crack, Eldorado Canyon, Boulder, Colorado. (*W. Piper*)

A wide stem enables the climber to reach the corner and secure a fist jam in the crack. (*R. Shaw*)

moved up onto the edge, the weight of the body is transferred over it, and the climber stands up. When the ledge is small or sloping outward and lacks a good sharp edge, the technique is similar but much more difficult. Frequently, a small leap may be needed to get the climber's upper body above the ledge. The body may be better sideways instead of facing the rock, and the climber may have to rest on one straight arm, while his other hand finds a hold above to help him onto the ledge. A windowsill of a suitable height is a good place to practice this technique. If the hold onto which you are mantelshelfing is a small one, additional pressure on it may be gained by placing one hand above the other. Often small holds may exist by which it is possible to avoid the mantelshelf.

When on a mantelshelf, it is important to resist the temptation to use your knees. You may find yourself kneeling on the ledge with no hold in reach above to pull you upright. An excellent position for prayer, but not for progress. Often on a cliff your upward progress will be barred by an overhang or a section of blank rock. Then it becomes necessary to **traverse;** that is, to move sideways on the rock without significant gain or loss in height. Traversing can be easier than climbing, in that you are not expending the energy to lift your body, only to move its position sideways. The sequence of holds should be worked out carefully as your feet will have to cross over as you move, especially on small holds. It is possible, if the handholds are good, to change feet on a small hold by hopping, that is moving one foot off and the other on in a quick movement. Usually it is better to step through to another hold rather than risk the jerky movement.

Occasionally when the cliff is steep it may be necessary to do a **hand traverse,** that is to hang by the hands and swing along from hold to hold, usually on a good edge of rock. Some modern climbs involve a hand traverse over a roof using hand jams in a crack. Again this maneuver is better carried out on straight arms. Very infrequently the climber comes across a situation where the pitch has to be negotiated lying on his stomach, or on his back. This occurs when an undercut ledge is topped by an overhang, such that the climber can neither stand on the ledge or use it as a handhold. Then the climber has to decide whether it would be better to move along the ledge on his face or on his back. Once in a situation like this, I made the wrong decision and inched along the ledge on my stomach until the ledge disappeared from view. At that point, with half my body projecting into space and only held there by a finger or two jammed at the back of the ledge, I discovered that there was no hold within my reach, and though I could see a good edge above me I could not turn. Moreover, due to the construction of the ledge I could not retreat. Eventually I solved the problem by fixing a runner and letting myself fall off the ledge. My second who came along on his back, laughing uproariously, had no problem.

In that situation I used the rope and a runner to solve a problem. A more orthodox use of the rope occurs during a **tension traverse.** Here, when the climber is confronted by a blank section of rock that he must cross, he fixes a good runner and edges his way across leaning on the rope that is inched out by his second. If you want to convince yourself that this will work, tie a rope between two trees a few feet above the ground. Only a skilled tightrope walker would be able to cross on it. Now fix another rope a few feet higher to one tree and you will find that, by maintaining tension on the hanging rope, you can walk, without too much difficulty, to the other tree. As the climber does this on rock he makes use of small side holds and wrinkles that would not be sufficient if he did not have tension on the rope.

Another possibility is to climb higher than the point you mean to cross, fix a runner, retreat, and then swing across to the place you want to reach. On your arrival you will have to find a hold quickly, or you will be snatched back by the angle of the rope. This technique is called a **pendulum traverse.** Sometimes to

A difficult mantelshelf on a steep pinnacle. The climber has protected himself with one of the ropes through a running belay at chest height. (*R. Shaw*)

A delicate traverse under a roof. (*S. Hilbert. Courtesy, Idaho State University, Outdoor Program*)

Even with no positive holds for the feet, a good undercling is very secure. (*J. Shaw*)

reach the required stance the climber has to get momentum up by running backward and forward on the face. Needless to say, the runner above must be sound.

When surmounting overhangs and bulges the most important technique is speed. Work out the sequence of holds before you start and keep moving over the out-of-balance section. Look for ways of cheating the overhang, that is, for holds that will enable you to stay in balance. When you put your feet on the holds keep to the outside edge if they are large enough. The farther out your feet are, the more you are in balance.

One specialized technique developed in the Shawangunks in New York is the use of a **heel hold.** Here the climber swings one foot above the overhang and jams his heel into a corner or onto a ledge. Then, with a swing, the body is brought up and toward the heel, and levered up.

The best way to improve your skill is to climb regularly and on as many different types of rock as possible.

An undercling with the right hand enables the climber to move left to a finger jam in the crack. Upper Cathedral Spire, Yosemite. (*R. Shaw*)

Chapter 10

INTERLUDE: YOSEMITE, CALIFORNIA

The crack looms steeply above us, clean and uncompromising. Starting is going to be difficult. About twenty feet from the ground the crack disappears and an overhang bars the entrance. We look around. A traverse into the crack from the right might be possible. Let's give it a try.

The rock is warm and my fingers sweat on the small rounded holds as I climb, balancing up with held breath until I am level with the crack. Rather nervous, as I often am on the first pitch, I fiddle around trying to slot a chock into a hairline crack. A waste of time. Nothing is working.

A step up, quivering, trying to push the drop out of my mind. Balance. Left hand gently groping, a hesitant spider toward the crack. Must move my feet. As though stepping on eggs, my left foot on a sloping fingernail of rock, I sway over. A good edge for the left hand. Right hand following and jamming deep into the crack and I'm over. Phew! Toes wedge in securely and hands feel firmly dug into the rough granite.

Up I go moving fast on the steep rock. No runner for a while or the pull on Jim will be wrong for the traverse. Fifteen feet up, the crack narrows. I stop, nose against the wall.

Jim smiles up from below. Far below. Fumbling on my rack I select a large wedge and it slots in as though custom-made. Rope clipped through and I relax, looking up. Ten feet to a good ledge. Crack too narrow for toe jams. Try one or two then retreat, puffing. No holds

on the wall. Must be a layback. An ant wanders past, disdainfully.

I reach up, lean back, and commit myself. The edge of the crack is not good, but I layback up it with a speed born of doubts about my finger strength. Fingers sliding on the hot rock. Chalk would be a help, but it seems such a cop-out and so messy.

A flurry of arms and legs and I'm on the ledge. A trickle of blood comes from a skinned finger. Must relax more. Be less hasty. Place my hands more carefully.

I belay to a super spike and a nut and bring Jim up. He climbs fearlessly with hardly a hesitation, and arrives smiling and breathing easily. Maybe I'm just getting old.

Jim takes the rack and leads on up a line of small holds beside the hairline crack. For a moment he straddles an overlap, black against the deep blue sky, then he is gone.

A breeze fans my cheek. Across the cliff a chough sweeps, emphasizing the exposure. The rope inches out. The green forests flow like a solidified wave up the valley.

Jim shouts down and I watch the rope snake up as I remove my belay. I climb the pitch reasonably well, relaxed with the rope above me, enjoying the dance from hold to hold. Rock was obviously designed to be climbed; why else would it have such perfection?

Back in the crack again, side jamming my toe and overlapping my fingers. Then I'm in the sentry box beside Jim, saying what a great

(*P. Ross*)

(P. Ross)

pitch it was and peering up timorously at the crack above. A bulge humps out above Jim's head and I tentatively move up onto it. Steep. Back I come to the security of the sloping sentry box, trying to smile. Up again. Back again. The bulge caps a small dihedral and suddenly I realize that minute holds are to be found on its walls. Up again, this time keeping out of the crack, legs straddled, thigh tendons stretching. Between my legs Jim looks up smiling, and far below him, like a bed of nails, the spiky tops of the pines.

Body over to the left above my foot. Pull with left hand on a small knob, push with right. Up. Right foot over and out to a sloping ledge. Straighten up. Beautiful spike for my right hand and I'm over.

The crack resumes, wider now and my boot has to wedge sideways. A large hexagonal chock eases my mind.

I'm climbing better. I can feel a bubbling happiness at the perfection of the climb, at the movement of my body poised above the drop, at the curl of my fingers over flakes and the firm hold of the crack on my bunched hand. Another good ledge, comfortable to sit on with legs dangling over the edge.

Then Jim is up again and away. We thread our way up past roofs, across ledges, leapfrogging through a maze of overhangs. Dancing delicately on slabs. Grunting on bulges. A groaning thrutch, stemming up a wide chimney. Subtle shades of lichen on steep walls with sharp incut holds. And then, sudden and delightful, the top. A light breeze stirs our hair and we sit gaping at cliffs and trees and sky endlessly stretching. Then boots loosened and carabiners and chocks clanking round our necks, we whoop our way down through the scented forest.

Chapter 11

EQUIPMENT AND CLOTHING FOR ICE CLIMBING AND MOUNTAINEERING

EQUIPMENT

The bone-chilling recesses of an ice filled couloir or the north face of Mount Rainier is a far cry from the sunbaked rock of Whitehorse Ledges or Tahquitz. The mountaineer and the ice climber must have good equipment to cope with these challenges.

If you have chosen your climbing boots wisely, they will also be suitable for general mountaineering including the ascent of glaciers and couloirs. If you intend to climb ice in the winter, a sport of growing popularity, you may need double boots to protect your feet from the hazards of frostbite. An excellent double boot is the Eastern Mountain Sports Assiniboine, or the Makalu Double Boot made by Galibier. Usually, however, a single boot with room for two pairs of socks, one thick and one thin, will be adequate. Much depends on how efficient your circulation is, or whether you are a smoker. Smoking, by constricting the peripheral blood vessels, increases the risk of frostbite.

The wearing of an efficient pair of gaiters can improve the warmth of your feet considerably since they trap a layer of air around your calf and boot. They also prevent snow and stones getting into the top of your boots and they keep your legs and feet dry.

In addition to a warm pair of boots, you will need crampons. It is possible to do without them, as mountaineers once did, by cutting steps with your ice axe, but their use greatly improves your safety and speed on the mountain. Few mountaineers would now venture out without them. For general mountaineering, one of the best pairs of crampons is the Salewa adjustable. These have twelve points and are fairly light and durable. The big advantage of these crampons is the ability to adjust them to fit any boot. So, when you have your boots resoled or buy a new pair, your crampons will still be of use. If your intention is to do high-angled technical ice climbs, you will probably need more rigid crampons. Among the best are S.M.C. rigid crampons or a Chouinard-Salewa pair. Both incorporate very rigid curved front points that are designed to bite well into steep water ice and not to vibrate, which would cause the ice to crack. Of the two, the Chouinard-Salewa are much lighter. This type of crampon must only be used with a rigid-sole boot as a more flexible boot will cause fatigue cracks to develop in the metal. When it comes to ice axes it is again important to decide what kind of ice climbing you intend to do. For the beginner who aims to do mountain climbs of a fairly easy technical standard involving glaciers and snow slopes a general purpose axe such as the M S R Thunderbird or Eagle is ideal. A fiberglass or metal-shafted axe is much better than a wooden one.

(R. Shaw)

An excellent pair of winter boots incorporating an inner boot. (*Courtesy, Recreational Equipment, Inc.*)

These Supergators are perfect for winter conditions since they are waterproof and warm and cover the boot securely down to the welt. (*Courtesy, The Great Pacific Iron Works*)

In general mountaineering, the axe is used for step cutting, that is, cutting small platforms for ascent and descent, belaying and self-arrest, and the design has to take account of these functions. (These techniques will be covered in detail in the following chapter.) The strength of the shaft is important when taking a fall. Equally important is the ability of the pick to bite into the ice during a self-arrest. The optimum hooking angle at the end of the pick appears to be about 68 degrees, and there should be a positive clearance angle on the other side from the direction of pull. Good axes are also made by Forrest Mountaineering. Their Neve model was used in the successful 1976 American Bicentennial Expedition to Everest. Their axes are very strong and well balanced. It is important to choose an axe with a reasonably heavy head to make step cutting easier.

The length of the axe is a matter of personal choice. My preference, for general mountaineering, is an axe whose spike will just touch the ground when the head is held in the hand with the body erect. Unlike some other climbers, I don't like to use the axe as a walking stick on fairly level or gently angled snow and find a larger axe an encumbrance on steep ground. On the other hand, descent is easier with a long axe to cut with.

For technical ice climbing, the choice is more difficult. A wide range of different designs of axe has recently become available. In technical ice climbing the climber carries two axes, or a hammer and an axe. On steep ice he swings the pick into the ice and moves up on

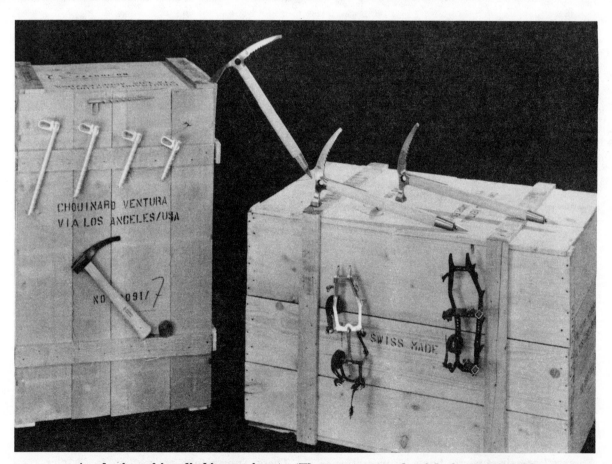

A selection of ice-climbing equipment. The crampon on the right is an adjustable one for general mountaineering and moderate ice climbing. Several tubular ice screws of different lengths, as displayed on the box at the left, are very useful. The piton hammer, below, has a spike that can be used to remove pitons or chop holds in ice. The wooden shafted axes on the box on the right are light to carry and can have an adze or a hammer head. (*Courtesy, The Great Pacific Iron Works*)

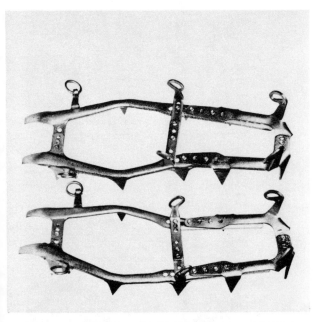

These adjustable rigid crampons are ideal for high-angle ice climbing, but demand a stiff boot. (*Courtesy, The Great Pacific Iron Works*)

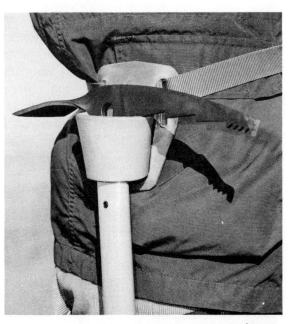

A holster can be extremely useful, especially when ascending mixed terrain. (*D. Hall. Courtesy, Forrest Mountaineering*)

Two of the best general-purpose ice axes manufactured in the U.S. They are metal-shafted with a chrome molybdenum head. The Névé model is for general mountaineering while the Verglas is superior on steep ice. (*D. Van Pelt. Courtesy, Forrest Mountaineering*)

The choice of technical ice axes is wide. The Serac Saber with its sharply drooping pick gives a secure placement in steep water ice. The axe can have a hammer head instead of an adze. (*D. Van Pelt. Courtesy, Forrest Mountaineering*)

the front points of his crampons. Steps are rarely cut in this situation. Until recently ice climbers cut hand- and footholds and moved up as though they were on rock, using one axe, usually fairly short. Now the climber maintains his balance on his front points and the pick of one axe, while the other axe pick is swung into the ice. This technique can be accomplished by using two short general-purpose axes with sharp picks, but it really comes into its own with the use of specialized tools. One of the early innovations was made by Hamish McInnes of Glencoe, Scotland, who designed an axe called a Terrordactyl. The axes are fifteen inches long and the pick has a 55-degree droop. They come with either an adze or a hammer head, and you should have one of each. Because of the extreme droop of the pick, there is a tendency to bang your knuckles on steep ice, but their holding power is superb. Other good axes for technical ice climbing include the Forrest Mjöllnir, which has interchangeable picks for different conditions, the Curver Axe produced by Snowdon Mouldings of Wales, the Simond Ice Hammer, the Eagle Ice Hammer made by Salewa, and the Hummingbird Ice Hammer made by Lowe Alpine Systems. My preference is for the McInnes Peck Terrordactyls, but it is vital that you try out a few of the varieties for yourself before buying. Most climbers would

In all short axes for technical ice climbing a wrist loop is essential as an added grip as well as to rest on. (*D. Hall. Courtesy, Forrest Mountaineering*)

The Mjöllnir Ice Hammer has interchangeable heads. Here it is shown with a tubular pick. Blade picks are also available with varying angles of droop. (*D. Van Pelt. Courtesy, Forrest Mountaineering*)

be prepared to let you use their axe to experiment and only a trial can let you know if the axe is to your liking.

Whereas the rock climber uses natural features or chocks to provide protection, the snow and ice climber usually relies on ice pitons and screws. For security, the tubular ice screw has the best holding power. The screw is hammered in until the threads catch, then turned using another screw, or the ice axe, as a lever. Ice pitons are simply hammered into the ice. A series of light blows prevents the ice from fracturing. Wherever possible the screw or piton be inserted at about a 60-degree angle to the slope. In this respect the placement is different from a rock piton, which may hold a considerable load even when at a downward angle. Generally, the use of screws has superseded ice pitons since they are more secure and easier to extract.

Another useful device for anchoring on

snow was developed from an anchor used for sled dogs. It consists of a light metal plate, like the blade of a shovel, with a wire sling attached. When it is driven into the snow and the belay is made to the wire sling, a pull will force the blade deeper into the snow. This belay is often called the deadman or snow fluke and provides a vastly superior anchor to the ice axe.

A down parka is vital survival clothing for a long winter or high-mountain climb. Dark glasses or snow goggles are essential to prevent eye damage through snow glare. A wool head covering should also be mandatory to prevent heat loss. (*Courtesy, Recreational Equipment, Inc.*)

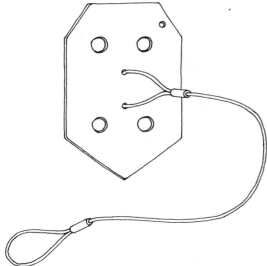

The snow fluke is a much safer anchor on snow than an ice axe. (*J. Shaw*)

CLOTHING

Clothing for ice climbing and mountaineering must of course be very efficient. On a day of bitter cold I once had to stand for five hours on a minute ice ledge while my friend led an exceptionally steep ice pitch. Now, with improved equipment and techniques you are unlikely to have to spend so long on one pitch, but the unpredictability of mountain weather and situations demand top-quality clothing. In addition to normal summer mountain wear, four other items of clothing are almost essential.

Almost 50 percent of heat loss from the body occurs through the head, so a head covering is vital. A wool balaclava, which can be worn under the climbing helmet is ideal.

Another popular item of clothing is the down parka. It has the advantage that it can be compressed into a stuff sack and carried until it is needed. On high-angle climbs, its bulkiness can interfere with movement, but its lightness and warmth are valuable in emergency situations. Several companies market sew-it-yourself kits which reduce the expense. It is worth considering a filling of less expensive synthetic fill, which has the advantage of retaining your heat while wet, but it does make the jacket a heavier and bulkier one.

Long underwear, or a one-piece undersuit,

For low-altitude winter climbing a waterproof parka with a down filling can be a useful combination. (*Courtesy, Nevisport*)

Wool is an ideal fabric since it retains its warmth when wet and adheres well to snow and ice holds. Fingerless gloves permit sensitivity on small holds and can be combined for added warmth with a wool mitt. (*D. Van Pelt. Courtesy, Forrest Mountaineering*)

For really severe mountain conditions clothing made in polyester pile gives excellent insulation. (*D. Hall. Courtesy, Forrest Mountaineering*)

can be used in combination with your normal summer mountaineering clothes to provide considerable warmth.

Like all the body's extremities, the hands are very vulnerable to frostbite. For ice climbing, wool is best as it remains warm when wet and adheres to icy holds. I find the best combination is a fingerless glove under a Dachstein mitt. The mitts can be removed for a short period if any delicate rock climbing has to be done. It is worthwhile putting a spare pair of mitts into your sack; the loss of a mitt on the mountain could have serious consequences.

Clothing should, in general, be readily adjustable. Even on very cold days, if you are working strenuously, you can become overheated. If you then sweat heavily, the resultant dampness will leave you much colder. Wear clothes that can be opened or taken off easily. Several layers provide more insulation and temperature control than one or two.

On mountains where you will be on snow

or ice for much of the time, it is essential to have some protection for your eyes to guard against snow blindness, which is a very painful complaint. Choose a pair of goggles that are lightweight, made of tinted glass, and are well ventilated. Some climbers prefer to use sunglasses and find them adequate.

A reliable head torch is invaluable. This should be lightweight and comfortable. Lithium batteries have come into use recently and are greatly superior to the older type. On many occasions, especially on winter ice climbs when the days are short, I have spent the night in a warm hut or tent, rather than an icy bivouac, because of a good head torch.

In mountaineering, good equipment makes a considerable contribution to safety. Never buy an inferior item just because it is cheaper. On the other hand, don't rush out and bankrupt yourself with the purchase of every piece of equipment in the store. It's better to acquire your gear slowly as you gain experience. While you do, climb with your friends, make use of things that they already have, and pick their brains as to what is the best to buy when you can afford to.

Chapter 12

ON THE MOUNTAIN: TECHNIQUES OF SNOW AND ICE CLIMBING

The ascent of most major mountains involves the surmounting of problems posed by snow and ice as well as by rock. The approach to the peak may be over a glacier, and the actual climb may follow a couloir of snow or ice or a ridge. The ability to move safely and quickly on such ground is an essential skill.

Before you venture on a mountain of any seriousness, you must spend a considerable amount of time becoming familiar with the use of your ice axe and crampons. Find a snow slope for practice that runs out at a gentle angle, so that if you lost control you would come to no harm. Look especially for any rocks protruding through the snow that would injure you if you slid into them.

The first thing to practice is the technique of self-arrest. It is vital, on a climb, that you be able to stop a slide instantly if you slip. This takes hours of practice but is essential before you venture farther.

Leave your crampons in the sack and take your axe, putting your gloved hand through the wrist loop. The axe should always be held so that your thumb is under the adze and the pick is facing backward. In this position you are immediately ready to arrest a slide. Get into the habit of holding your axe like this even on easy terrain. Climb up the slope for about a hundred feet, kicking your boots into the snow and driving the point of the axe in

above and to the side of you. When you have climbed far enough for a good but safe slide, move to the side away from your line of steps, and kick a good ledge where you can relax and take the weight off your calves.

Now you are going to slide back down to the bottom. Hold the axe with your right hand on the head. Your thumb lies under the adze. The axe is then held at an angle across your body with your left hand low down on the shaft at a level with your left hip. The head of the axe is just by your right shoulder. (Left-handed climbers will obviously reverse these directions.) With a good firm grip on the axe lie face down on the snow and allow yourself to slide.

Braking is effected by gently pressing the pick into the snow. You will find that you come to rest very easily, unless the snow is rock hard or very powdery. In the latter situation, it may be advisable to reverse the axe and use the broad blade of the adze for braking. Practice this position until you are absolutely confident in your ability to stop within a few feet after a short slide.

When you are happy with the feel of the axe, start off in a sitting position and roll over onto your stomach once a good speed has been attained. In the sitting position, hold the axe at the ready so that the only movement needed is a roll onto your face. Be careful not

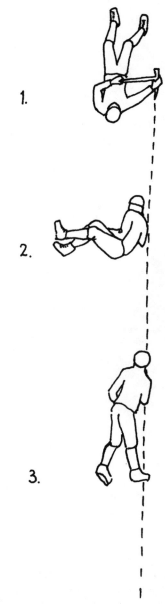

The correct position for the ice axe when arresting a slip. (*J. Shaw*)

to drive the pick too suddenly into the snow or it may be jerked from your grasp. Again, work at this position until you can stop quickly, even from a fast slide.

Often if a fall develops on snow the climber will slide head first, so you need experience of an arrest from this position. It is better when practicing head-first positions to use a rope for safety, unless the slope is absolutely safe. If you are using a rope, fix it securely to two anchors, one at the top of the slope and the other about halfway down, and leave a loop of slack below the bottom anchor. Then clip into the rope with a carabiner on your harness so that you are free to slide.

It is better to have a partner to launch you into the head-first slide. Make a ledge on which you can rest your shoulders while you maneuver your feet uphill. Start by lying on your face, so that the only body shift you have to accomplish is to get your feet below your

Self-arrest from a head-first slide. The first action is to bite the pick *gently* into the snow to one side (1). The body pivots around the axe (2) and comes into the self-arrest position (3). (*J. Shaw*)

head. This is done by pivoting your body around the pick. As you slide, place it in the snow to your side and, as it catches, your body will swing round it. If you perform the brake too violently, the axe may easily be jerked from your hands since the momentum of your body is considerable.

A steep ice gully in bad condition. The climber has to rely on rock belays for security. (*R. Shaw*)

On your back with your head downhill is not a pleasant position, and it is easy to feel disorientated. The braking movement is the same as the previous one. The pick is inserted into the snow to your right side and the body pivots round it to come into the feet-down braking position. In all these maneuvers the axe is held firmly across the body.

The two latter self-arrest techniques should be first practiced at the bottom of the slope and only tried at a higher point when confidence and technique are gained.

Once all these techniques have been perfected, try launching yourself on the slope in a variety of ways. When a slide develops it is rarely simple. The more experience you have of tumbling down a safe slope, the better able

you will be to arrest a real fall. Remember always that you are carrying a dangerous weapon, and treat its sharp edges with respect.

Many climbers have been injured during a fall because they lost the axe. Though some climbers disagree, I feel that a wrist sling should always be used. It gives a greater security to the hold of the right hand, though against its use is the fact that if your hold on the axe is lost, it can flail dangerously about your head.

If the ice axe is lost during a slide, it is still possible to self-arrest. This technique, too, should be practiced until, like the others, it becomes second nature. The braking position is the same, but without the axe the secret is to push the arms out stiffly, lifting the body from the snow. The weight of the body is then put onto the toes and can be sufficient to stop the slide, or at the least, to slow it. The principle is the same as that involved in climbing a slope; the closer you lean to the slope the easier it is to slide down.

I also recommend that you try a self-arrest with crampons. The problem here is that the spikes will bite into the snow and the body may well pivot around the feet in a backward roll. The knees have to be bent to keep the crampons out of the snow and the braking done entirely by the axe. It is often not easy to stop when wearing crampons. As in the other techniques, practice is vital.

The techniques of self-arrest lead naturally into the practice of glissading. This is a method of descending a snow slope by sliding, sitting down or, more comfortably, standing. It is an exhilarating experience, but regrettably very dangerous. There was a time in the first few years of my climbing life when I hardly ever made a descent without a long glissade. However, as the years went by and an ever-growing number of my friends had been injured glissading, I gave up the practice. Well, not completely. Now I only glissade down a slope I know very well or one that I have ascended. Even then there is a risk as the snow conditions can change from day to day and, also, with a drop in altitude, so it is almost impossible to predict what you will meet with in a long glissade. One moment you may be in complete control on firm old snow, the next your pick may be slicing through a windcrust with as much stopping power as a hot knife in butter.

For the record, though as I emphasize I do not recommend it, the sitting glissade is performed with the axe as for the self-arrest, with the pick slowing the glissader down in the snow just above the hip. A standing glissade is accomplished by using the feet as in skiing, descending in a steep diagonal, sideslipping and edging the boots, while using the spike of the axe behind to control and stabilize.

Now that we have hurled ourselves about on the snow until the point is reached where

Single-axe technique on moderately angled ice. Notice how the boot is placed for the maximum bite by the crampons. The axe is held in the self-arrest position. (*Courtesy, Yosemite Curry Company*)

we can arrest a slip instantly, we are ready to practice ascending and descending steeper slopes. It is best to start without crampons. Like all equipment crampons are subject to failure and it is worth being familiar with techniques without them. Try moving up a steep slope by kicking your boots into the snow. If it is hard, you may only be able to make a small step with a single kick. The technique is to plant your axe, spike down, into the snow, kick into the snow with one foot, step up, kick in with the other foot, step up; then, in balance, withdraw your axe and plant it again. It is best to advance diagonally, making a larger step at each change in direction. Always move methodically and rhythmically, pausing as the axe is withdrawn and replaced. The first principle in all climbing is conservation of energy.

If the slope is steeper, the axe can be held across the body and the spike thrust into the snow almost horizontally. On a snow slope above about 50 degrees the pick, rather than the spike of the axe, is used. It is forced into the snow with the axe held in the self-arrest position.

In all these methods of ascent there comes a point at which the climber has to balance and withdraw the axe. This calls for good balance, especially if the snow is hard or crampons are

Good balance is important when using a single axe on steep snow. It works best on firm snow ice where little force is necessary to sink the pick. (J. Shaw)

Movement on steeper snow. A foothold is kicked into the snow and the spike of the axe is planted firmly above the climber. The last climber should be belaying the second climber's rope. On steep snow it is safer for all members of a party to be belayed at all times. (Courtesy, Mount Adams Wilderness Institute)

An instructor teaching the single-axe technique. (*Courtesy, Mount Adams Wilderness Institute*)

Ascent of an ice bulge using two axes and crampon front points. The two-axe technique gives great speed on long moderately steep mountain slopes, though most climbers prefer tools of a uniform size and more-steeply angled picks. (*Courtesy, Lute Jerstad Adventures*)

not being worn. This has led to the development of two-axe technique. (They are only of use on steep slopes, the second axe being an encumbrance when the angle is gentle.) With the axes held in your hands, with the thumb under the adze and the fingers over the head, the picks can be used as daggers. Using this method there is no point at which there is the insecurity of removing the axe while you have no other support for your hands. Very rapid progress can be made using two axes, and

there is the added bonus that if one is lost, you are still able to negotiate snow and ice slopes using the other.

Without crampons, and sometimes with them, it is essential to be able to cut steps. Old snow, after thawing and freezing several times, may become so hard that even several kicks with a boot will barely mark it.

When chopping steps, let the axe do the work. Make sure that you are secure and swing the adze decisively, with the whole arm, at the snow. Aim to cut the step with the first swing and only make it as large as necessary, except when a change in the diagonal is planned. Work out where the step is to be and do not over stretch. As you will be moving diagonally most of the time, the hold you are fashioning is for the edge of the boot. It wants to be about six inches in length. The steeper the snow, the more important it is to make the step slope back from the lip. This is especially so when you are moving up high-angle snow and are using the holds as handholds.

If the snow is very hard, or if you are on ice, you may have to cut with the pick rather than the adze. In this situation you will need several blows to cut the step. The first blow should not be too hard or the pick may embed itself.

All step cutting is very tiring, and on steep ice can be exhausting and time consuming. The climber may have to retire to a ledge or insert a piton to rest. Every use should be made of alternatives. It may be better to take a longer route to make use of projecting rocks, both for holds and protection. In a couloir, the edge of the ice may be melted by the rock and provide an easier and safer route. It is a good principle in snow and ice climbing to keep as close to rock as possible. Anchors in snow and ice, as we shall see, are often very poor, whereas a good piton, nut, or natural belay on rock will reduce the danger markedly.

With crampons, much of the labor is taken out of snow climbing. On hard snow, where several blows with the uncramponed boot would be needed to gain a small hold, the spikes of the crampon will bite with little effort into the snow to give a secure footing. Moreover, using two short axes like daggers, climbers wearing crampons can race up fairly steep snow, leaving greater time for the more technically difficult sections.

The placement of feet in crampons obviously needs care, especially in descent. A carelessly placed foot can snag on your pants and lead to a fall. Moreover, in certain snow conditions, snow can ball up under the cram-

This glacier on Mount Hood provides a wide variety of ice situations for the perfection of techniques. (*Courtesy, Lute Jerstad Adventures*)

pon and result in dangerous instability. Many climbers fix plastic sheet under their crampons to repel the build up of snow.

In recent years, the technique of ascending very steep ice has been perfected using short axes with curved or angled picks, and rigid crampons. The conventional method of climb-

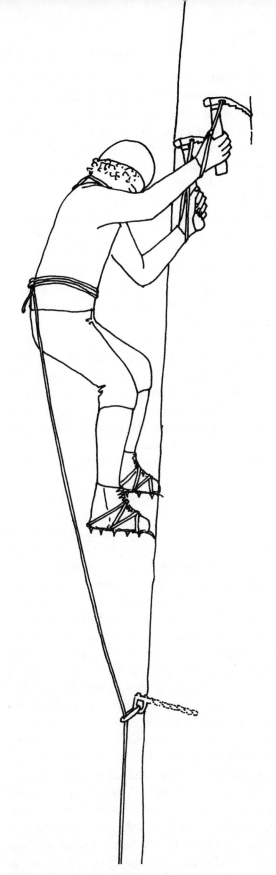

ing steep ice was to cut pigeon-hole hand- and footholds and for the climber to ascend, holding on to the lower holds while the upper ones were cut. When he became tired the climber would either rest on an ice piton or screw, or descend to a resting place. This meant that progress was slow. An important feature of this technique is to work out quickly where the ideal hold placements are and cut them with the minimum of effort.

The modern technique involves little cutting. Instead, the climber swings the angled pick of the short axe or hammer into the ice above his head, holds on, and places the other axe beside it but far enough away to spread the load on the ice. He then crampons up until his hand on the shaft of the axe is about shoulder level. Resting on the front points of his crampons and the pick of one axe, he removes the other and swings it in at full stretch above him. Holding on to that he removes the second axe, places it beside the higher one, and then proceeds. The strain on his hands is eased by strong wrist loops. Remember that it is essential to rest on a straight arm.

All climbing on steep ice, whether by hold cutting or by two-axe technique, demands considerable fitness and strength. It is also essential that the points of the crampons and the pick of the axe be kept filed sharp.

On water ice the points of the crampon are placed rather than banged into the ice. Too violent a kick and the ice will shatter or the boot rebound. A gentle thrust places the front points of the crampon so that they are level, then the climber puts weight on to them keeping the boot horizontal. Any deviation from the horizontal by the boot will tend to lever the points out or to shatter the ice. Like most climbing actions, the movements should be performed positively and smoothly. Do not neglect the fact that ice is rarely uniform; small wrinkles on the surface can make the hold more secure and the other points of the crampon can be employed.

Often, during an ascent, a section of rock will have to be negotiated in crampons, either

Rigid boots and crampons are needed for steep snow. (*J. Shaw*)

because there is no time to remove them or because, as in the middle of a pitch, it is impossible. Your first experience of this is likely to be fairly nerve wracking, but you will soon find that crampons provide a surprisingly good hold on rock.

Place the points of your crampons carefully, choosing flat or incut holds, though smaller, in preference to larger sloping holds. The front points of the crampon generally provide greater security than the side points. It is probably less of a strain leading on rock in crampons than it is being a second out of sight, and having to listen to the scratching and scraping of the leader!

Belaying on snow and ice requires great care. Wherever possible use a rock belay. Though I rarely use pitons on pure rock climbs, I carry a selection in winter or on mountains for this eventuality. Chock placements may be found also, but frequently the best cracks are choked with ice.

If a natural rock or piton belay cannot be found, then an anchor may have to be made using an ice piton. Ice screws are preferable to ice pitons and their development has made the ice piton virtually obsolete. They are easier to insert, do not fracture the ice as readily, and can be extracted without difficulty. Some screws are tubular and are very useful for brittle ice. Other types, like the Chouinard Warthog, are hammered into the ice and unscrewed on removal. Carry a wide selection and practice with them before they are to be used in earnest. Any rotten ice should be cleared away first, then the screw is driven in at about 60 degrees to the slope.

Natural features on ice may provide belays. An edge or flake of ice can be notched to take a sling or the climbing rope. Alternatively, a bollard can be cut in ice or hard snow. In ice, the bollard should be about two feet in diameter, and a trench of at least six inches should be cut at the back to take the rope. In snow the dimensions should be doubled. The anchor in snow can be strengthened by padding the rope with clothing, or by running the rope behind an embedded ice axe.

On snow, perhaps the best belay is the deadman or snow fluke. This metal plate is about a foot square with a three-foot wire strop attached centrally. A slot is cut in the snow and the plate is inserted at an angle of about 45 degrees to the slope. A second slot, forming a "T" with the first, is cut for the wire sling. The sling should be extended by the addition of another sling to set the deadman as far back from the edge of the slope as possible; at least six feet of sling is best. The ice axe may also be buried like a deadman with a sling attached to the shaft. Since its surface area is much less, an axe is not nearly as effective as a deadman.

The axe can also be used as an anchor driven into the slope at an angle of about 70 degrees. Ice-axe belays are very suspect in snow and should be used only if there is no alternative. The anchor will be improved if someone can stand on the head of the axe, or if several axes are linked.

When belaying on snow and ice, the anchor should be fixed well above the stance, so that the pull on the anchor is as little as possible outward. The technique, when about to take a belay, is to look for a lessening of the angle and cut a good-sized ledge, then to climb about ten feet higher to place the anchor. Several well-spread anchors should be linked with slings, then the climber, having clipped in, descends to the ledge. The rope to the second is taken in, in the normal way, round the waist or through a belay plate. If several anchor placements can be found, the second's rope, if he is to lead through, should run through the top screw on a carabiner. When reaching the top of a climb, where the angle changes from the near vertical to the near horizontal, move well back from the lip before belaying, as snow lips can collapse without much warning.

Often on long mountain routes it is essential that the party move together on moderately angled snow and ice. If the stretch is a long one, it is probably better to unrope and move as individuals assuming that the party is a competent one. If this is felt to be unwise, then each climber carries some coils of rope in

The traditional axe belay. Not nearly as satis-factory as the snow fluke on a serious climb. Keep the axe as high above you as you can and use a sitting belay where possible. (*J. Shaw*)

Use an ice-axe belay only when the snow condi-tions are good. Parties moving quickly rely a lot on axe belays for speed. (*J. Shaw*)

It is important to belay well back from the lip of a snow slope. (*Courtesy, Mount Adams Wilderness Institute*)

his hand so that the climbers are about thirty feet apart.

Eternal vigilance is essential when moving together, as a slip by one member may land the party in disaster. The ice axe is always held ready to plunge into the snow, and the rope to the other climber should be already round the shaft, held in place by the fingers of the hand on the axe. If a slip occurs the belayer rams the axe into the snow and sinks on top of it with foot, knee, or body. This is essential or the axe may be plucked from the snow by the belay rope. When braking a falling climber using this method, the rope should be allowed to slide and only brought gradually to a halt. A refinement of this belay that requires less practice is to fix a short sling to the head of the axe and clip a carabiner through the sling. The rope is then twisted once round the carabiner. If a fall occurs, the axe is driven into the snow as before but the rope runs through the carabiner, not round the shaft. The advantage to this method is that the rope is always ready to belay and cannot become detached from the axe, and the friction provided by the turn around the carabiner will produce a gradual slowing of the fall.

These latter belaying techniques are essential for glacier crossing. On a glacier, for most of the time, the party will be moving together. It is vital always to use a rope on a snow-covered glacier even if the terrain is easy because of the possibility of crevasses. A party of three or four is preferable to a pair when crossing a crevassed glacier, since the extra numbers will help to arrest a fall and expedite the rescue of a climber in a crevasse. With a pair of climbers, it is better to operate at a distance of about forty feet. The climbers should tie on, leaving that gap between them and coil the excess rope at the ends around their shoulders and tie it off. Each climber should have two prusik loops already tied on the rope. As they move across the glacier the climber behind controls the rope, taking in and letting run coils, leaving about twenty feet between him and the leader. Should the leader fall into

Practice is essential if the skill of ascending a rope using prusik loops is to be mastered. (*J. Shaw*)

a crevasse, the second arrests his fall with an ice-axe belay. Then, while the fallen climber stands in the prusik loops to take the weight off his body, the second makes the belay fast to the axe. The spare rope around his shoulder can now be unwound and dropped to the hanging climber. Wherever possible the ropes should be padded to prevent their cutting into the lip of the crevasse. The hanging climber ties on to the dropped end of rope and, with assistance from it if necessary, climbs the other rope using the prusik loops. Three prusik loops are preferable to two, the third one being placed around the climber's chest to help his balance. It is much easier to prusik up a rope if it is taut, so the hanging climber should, if possible, attach his climbing sack by a carabiner to the rope below him.

If the climber in the crevasse is unconscious or unable to help himself, the situation with a party of two is desperate. If the other climber has two ice axes and some pulleys, it may be possible to raise the hanging climber, but it is extremely unlikely. Consequently, a party of three should be regarded as essential for crossing any dangerously crevassed glacier.

During the crossing, the party should cut across the crevasses at right angles. The crevasse may be crossed by jumping at a narrow point, by traversing until it can be bypassed, or by negotiating a snowbridge. The latter is the most dangerous method, especially if the temperature is above freezing. It is often the case that bridges crossed in the early morning, on the way to a climb, may collapse in the evening if recrossed. It is better

A party crossing a snowbridge over a large crevasse. On relatively easy terrain such as this the party moves together carrying loops of rope. (*Courtesy, Mount Adams Wilderness Institute*)

A crevasse being used for climbing practice. Note how the walls typically bulge, making exit difficult. (*Courtesy, Lute Jerstad Adventures*)

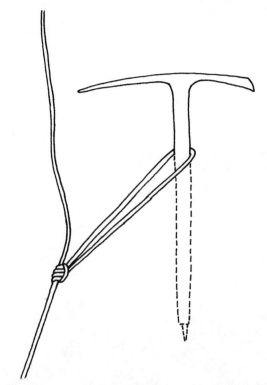

A sling may be fixed to the axe and a prusik knot attached to the rope, so that the rope may be hauled up and then held by the knot. (*J. Shaw*)

for the leader to cross a snowbridge on belay from the rest of the party, rather than for the party to continue to move together.

Many of the hazards of snow and ice on the mountains are due to shifts in temperature. That is why an early start is advisable on all mountain climbs to ensure an early return before snowbridges collapse, seracs fall, and stones, loosened by the sun, thunder down couloirs.

The principle of descending snow and ice is the same as for descending rock: face outward until the slope is too steep for comfort. The crampons should be placed, toe down, with as much of the sole in contact as possible. On gentle slopes the best action is a loping one, half bouncing from one foot to the other. This action sinks the crampon positively into the hard snow. The axe is carried across the body, held by both hands in the arrest position, ready to stop a fall. On steeper ground it will be necessary to traverse, using the spike of the axe as in the ascent. Steps may have to be cut to assist the descent. When the slope becomes steeper still, it is better to face in to the mountain and use the two-axe technique, moving down rhythmically and methodically.

If the slope is too steep to climb down confidently, a rappel may be fixed using a rock anchor if possible, or if not ice or snow bollards or screws. The rappel should be made as gently as you can, and the first climber down should be safeguarded by a safety rope, if one is available, from a separate anchor.

Most accidents occur on the descent of a mountain, mainly because the party has seen the summit as being the end of the difficulties and have relaxed their concentration. Moreover, at the end of the day, minds and bodies are tired and mistakes are easily made. The time to relax is when you are sitting with a mug of coffee back at base.

Despite its dangers and its discomforts, climbing on snow and ice can be the most enjoyable element of the sport. Even a small mountain can seem like a giant when clothed in ice, and even an easy route can give immense satisfaction.

Chapter 13

INTERLUDE: BEN NEVIS, SCOTLAND

Above me, George rested, his legs splayed out at a wide angle. Most of his crampon points were visible poised ten feet from my head. I cowered closer to the rock, trying to calculate how I would avoid him if he fell.

Below me, the black gash of the gully dropped onto a steep snow slope running to the valley. My feet felt like ice blocks, and my gloved fingers around the rope were stiffening. This was stupid. There was no way we were going to get up this gully. Twenty feet above George, the narrow gash was capped by an immense overhang, festooned with icicles like a giant's beard. The walls on either side looked blank for fifteen feet. Perhaps we could swing out on the rope to gain a precarious footing on the steep wall, but I was in no mood for that. Far below in the hut our friends would be drinking coffee and playing cards. I wanted to be with them. George started to move again, his crampons grating on the bare rock of the left wall, the sparks visible against the black rock. Chips of ice cascaded past my ears as he cut a hold. Oh come down, come down, George, I begged silently. The rope snaked up as he moved rhythmically, delicately, his red down jacket a splash of color against the black roof.

"How's it going?" I shouted, hearing a slight quaver in my voice.

"Okay," he grunted. "It doesn't look as though it'll go."

"Can you manage to come down?" I asked anxiously.

(*P. Ross*)

Silence. He moves up farther, the rope hanging free by my face and swaying in the wind. I think of the numerous rappels we will have to reach the bottom. But anything, anything to get out of this dark chasm.

Suddenly George laughs, an unexpected sound that sends my nerves jangling.

"There's a way through. It's only a huge chockstone. I can squeeze behind it."

He disappears, improbably, into the depths of the chimney. Large chunks of ice whistle past while I weave and dodge. Retreat is out. George has his mettle up and there's no stopping him. A shout tells me he has belayed and I resign myself to the ascent. Cold from standing, I fumble with ropes and carabiners then set off, clumsily. What George had danced up, I grunt and groan over, crampons skating off small holds. The stretch to reach both sides of the chimney in a bridging movement almost defeats me. The overhang looms nearer. If I come off, I'll swing with a crash into the back of the crack.

Then, with an inelegant scramble and a squeeze, I'm through, emerging from the black icy hole onto a wall of white steep snow bathed in sunlight. A trickle of sweat runs down my nose. George is above on a ledge grinning. When I reach him I find that there is little to grin about. He is belayed to an ice axe driven to the hilt in the snow at the back of the ledge. We are perched like flies on a great wall of white. Above, the slope stretches in grooves at about 70 degrees to the sky.

No better belay can be found, so I set off in trepidation, but at least warm from the sun and my exertions. My crampons bite with a satisfying crunch into the snow. I have two short axes, but one is in my sack and I can't be bothered to get it out. Up I go, pick of the axe driven above me; kick left foot, up; kick right foot, up; balance, remove the axe, and replant it above.

Below my heels George, still grinning, looks up. I run out sixty, seventy feet then begin to feel the drop below. The slope continues steeply above. I think of that one short axe on which everything depends. A slip now and George would be plucked with a jerk from his stance.

To my right I see an edge of rock protruding from the snow. I might get a runner on it. I edge over and up toward it. Five feet below

(*R. Shaw*)

(R. Shaw)

it I sense a change in the snow. My boot sinks in, as though into wet sugar. I feel a hold give beneath me. The rock, absorbing the sun, has melted the snow around it.

A good spike about eight feet higher leers at me. Once there and I would be safe, but to get there means climbing this rotten snow. Then I get an idea. I'll lasso the spike.

Balancing on my front points I remove my wrist loop and stick my axe in the snow by my face. Then gingerly, I coil some rope in my right hand. Pressed against the slope I throw the coils upward. They miss. Infinitely worse, they catch on the adze of my axe, jerk it out and send it falling, bouncing over the lip of the cliff below me.

For a second I sway on my holds. The space around me expands and I feel weak. Keep calm, keep calm. My right foothold suddenly settles an inch or two with a heart-stop-

ping crunch. Quickly I gather some more coils in my right hand, while my left tensely grips a small edge of snow. I throw once more and this time the loop slips neatly over the spike. I breathe again, then, supported by the rope, I get the other axe from my sack and climb on, putting a large runner on the spike as I pass.

Thirty feet farther on over an ice bulge where I managed to place a screw, I belay. Two hundred feet of straightforward climbing leads to the summit. George and I swing up it relishing the long drop below our feet, the warmth of the sun, and our companionship, the crunch of axe and crampon, and the blue winter's day.

Below us the gash which has swallowed my ice axe still lurks, dark and unpleasant, but already, in our minds, with the cold and uncertainty forgotten, becoming a place where we earned enjoyment.

Chapter 14

IN THE HIGH MOUNTAINS

Though the skills involved in climbing a short rock face or doing a technical ice climb on a waterfall are the same as those needed in making an ascent of a high mountain, there are still other factors that must be considered on a mountain climb.

Perhaps the most important is the weather. It is important to familiarize yourself with the pattern of weather in the area you intend to climb. Each mountain area has its own peculiarities of weather. Where you can, take heed of the weather forecast. At high altitude bad weather may be very unpleasant and dangerous. The ascent of a simple rock ridge can become a desperate struggle in a blizzard.

In addition to obtaining a forecast and learning what you can about the weather usual in the area, you should, of course, keep an eye out for a change. Temperature changes are especially important. A rise in temperature together with an increase in cloud often foretells a storm. Cold clear nights usually promise good weather; warm cloudy ones, especially if the moon develops a halo, portend bad conditions. Mountains often attract the discharge of lightning and in many areas thunderheads build up during the day to give an electrical storm in the afternoon.

If you are caught in a thunderstorm, make your way as quickly as possible off ridges and summits. One of the most frightening experiences of my life was being on a hard rock

A deep crevasse on the Rusk Glacier. (*Courtesy, Mount Adams Wilderness Institute*)

ridge with no escape, with rain cascading down it and lightning flashing incessantly around the mountain. Warning signs of the approach of lightning can be a buzzing sound from carabiners and pitons, or your hair may begin to stand on end. Lightning always takes the shortest path from the summit to earth, so avoid sheltering in cracks. It is not thought to be good practice to shelter in a hollow or under an overhang because the discharge may jump across the gap and burn anyone between. Probably the best course is to find a spot on the flank of a ridge and to sit on your rope or climbing sack. At one time, the advice was to get rid of all metal objects, but it is now thought that these play little part in attracting the lightning, and it is better to retain them for later use.

Of greater importance than the danger of lightning is that of avalanche. An avalanche is a mass of snow or ice sliding down a mountainside. It may begin as a relatively small slide, but increase in size and power as it descends. It is among the most unpredictable of mountain hazards, and a full-scale avalanche can wipe out villages. An avalanche can result from a variety of conditions, both warm and cold. We can divide avalanches into two types, the new-snow and the old-snow avalanche, though the slide may involve a combination of factors.

New-snow avalanches occur when there has been a recent fall of snow, making its stability most suspect. Much depends on the terrain under the snow. If it is rough and broken, the danger is lessened, but if, for example, the new snow falls on high-angled ice, the slide may be considerable. The new snow may adhere sufficiently until its equilibrium is disturbed by a climber crossing or ascending it. Always beware of deep new snow, though it is somewhat less dangerous if it is dry and powdery than if it is wet. You should generally avoid climbing a mountain after any recent snowfall.

Old-snow avalanches are less predictable. The most common type is due to a rapid thaw affecting a slope of high-angle snow. Once,

when some friends and I had almost completed a high-angle ice route, a sudden rise in temperature forced us to abandon the couloir and force a route onto a nearby ridge. The deep snow in the couloir became like porridge, and we could see and hear it begin to show signs of moving. Another danger in these conditions is that cornices at the top of the couloir will collapse and sweep down bringing other snow with it. A sudden rise in temperature on a snow route demands a rapid withdrawal or exit onto rock.

Another dangerous type of old-snow avalanche is a windslab avalanche. In this case the dry snow which has fallen some time before in cold conditions has not adhered to the ground beneath. Over a period of time, the top layer of it may thaw and freeze forming a hard icy crust that insulates the powder beneath. Eventually the weight of the upper crust may cause it to slide or the action of climbers, especially on a traverse, may break the support of a large slab. If avalanche conditions are suspected and no escape onto rock is possible, the party should not move together, even on easy ground. Secure belays should be taken and the leader should make full runouts with the rope.

If caught in an avalanche, probably the only hope is to try to swim with the flow and attempt to keep an air space around your mouth as the avalanche slows. Climbers have survived in avalanches for some time, so rapid action by the survivors or rescuers may save lives. Vigilance, common sense, and knowledge of local conditions are needed if one is to avoid the avalanche hazard.

Rockfall is another risk the mountaineer has to be aware of. It is caused usually by a change in the weather or by another party on the mountain. Cold weather followed by a thaw will work rock loose. Ice forming in cracks expands and fractures the rock. The rock is held together by the ice until the thaw comes. Consequently, if the weather is warm on a mountain, routes exposed to rockfall should be avoided. It is often possible to see where previous rockfall has occurred by scars

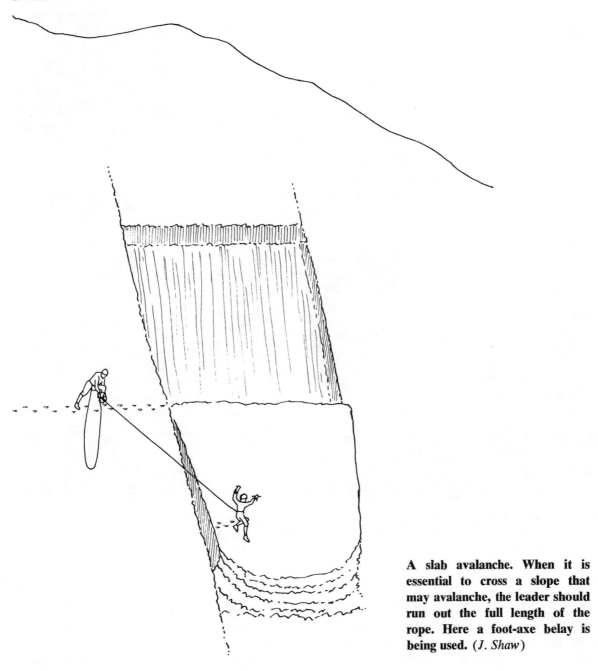

A slab avalanche. When it is essential to cross a slope that may avalanche, the leader should run out the full length of the rope. Here a foot-axe belay is being used. (*J. Shaw*)

on the rock or debris on the snow. Always be aware of the possibility of a party above you dislodging rocks. This is especially likely on a descent route where rappels are made. After the descent of a gully from a peak in the French Alps, my wife and I foolishly sat on the steep glacier below the gully to put on our crampons. From above came a terrifying rumble and shouts of warning. Large rocks smashed into the ice around us, but luckily we escaped.

During a descent always seek protection close to the sides of a gully and under overhangs, and at the bottom do not linger in the line of fire. It also goes without saying that the greatest care must be taken to avoid dislodging rocks yourself. Feet and hands should be placed carefully even on easy ground and

Descent of Chair Peak in the North Cascades, Washington. On an easy section of a descent or ascent, it is usual to keep the rope on and move together carrying coils. (*R. Shaw*)

the rope should be watched closely, especially when it is being retrieved from a rappel. Climbing helmets should always be worn on the mountain. Even on a simple mountain a "white out" can be a frightening experience. A white out occurs when, during a blizzard or thick mist, the light from the sky is diffused and casts no shadows on the snow. It is impossible to see the contour of a slope and to tell if one step in front of you is firm snow or a precipice. If you have knowledge of the mountain and are confident of your exact position, you can use your map and compass to find your way down. Even with a map and com-

pass, to proceed will expose you to the chance of a fall over small irregularities on the slope. The best procedure is to rope up and to belay each other. As the leader advances he puts his axe into the snow in front of him, using it as a blind person uses a cane. Throwing a spare axe on a long sling as you advance may also give your eyes a reference point. Everything depends on meticulous navigation. If the mountain is complex, the best plan is to stay put until the weather changes.

For this and other reasons you should always be prepared for a bivouac when on a mountain route. Of course, a balance has to be struck between carrying enough to weather any emergency and being totally unprepared. Too much equipment can slow the party down to the extent that a bivouac is inevitable.

Usually, on a long day climb on a serious mountain I carry a reserve of food, chocolate and nuts, and a down parka. Down has the great advantage that it is light and can be compressed into a small stuff sack. In addition I pack a long nylon waterproof anorak which will go over the parka and cover the knees. An excellent tool for survival is a large plastic bag big enough to get the entire body, except the head, in. The head has to be kept out as there is a danger of asphyxiation. Wind is the killer on a mountain. Considerable cold can be tolerated in calm conditions, but in a wind the body loses heat rapidly. Your efforts on an enforced bivouac should be directed to finding shelter from the wind.

A snow hole can be dug in the bank of a gully. The deadman anchor can be a useful tool here; some types are designed to be lashed to an ice axe to make a shovel. When digging a snow hole keep the exit as low as possible. Once the hole has been excavated an air hole can be made above it and the en-trance to the hole blocked off with snow blocks or your sack.

Since the digging of a snow hole even with shovels can be a lengthy task select the site with care. If you are unable to dig into a bank or under a cornice, you may have to dig a trench. It will be difficult to find a spot where the depth of snow is satisfactory and where the snow is soft enough to dig quickly, but in an emergency even a shallow trench is better than nothing.

In the mountains the treatment of injuries follows the same principles as in civilization except that specialized help and equipment is usually unobtainable. Every mountaineer should possess a good knowledge of first aid and its application to mountain accidents. First-aid information is beyond the scope of this book. I recommend that you acquire and study a book such as *Medicine for Mountaineering* (see Appendix 6), published in Seattle, Washington, by The Mountaineers. Three medical conditions are most common in mountain environments: frostbite, exposure, and altitude problems. Frostbite is serious cold injury to body tissues usually on exposed or peripheral areas such as fingers, toes, or the

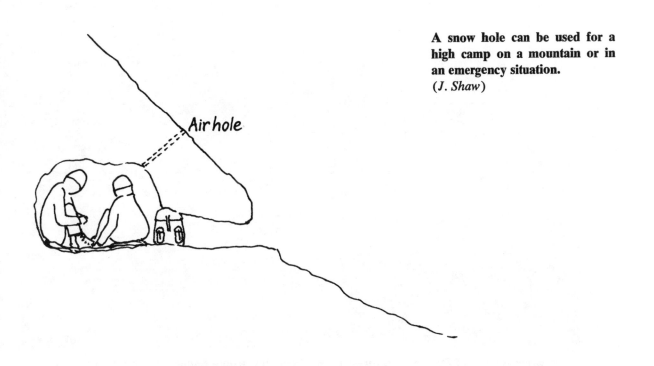

A snow hole can be used for a high camp on a mountain or in an emergency situation.
(*J. Shaw*)

Nearing the top of Dark Star Buttress in the Palisades. Route finding on mountain faces can be critical. (*Courtesy, Palisades School of Mountaineering*)

face. The blood vessels to the area constrict and the tissues die. At one time, due to the feared onset of gangrene, amputation was common. The modern treatment in the field is to keep the affected part warm by insulation. Any action that increases the circulation to the tissue without breaking the skin will help. Alcohol is the best drug as it opens up the capillary blood vessels. On no account should the victim be allowed to smoke. An excellent inexpensive booklet *Frostbite: Emergency Treatment,* published by The Museum of Science, Boston, by Bradford Washburn, details the most modern treatment. It is stocked by many ski and mountaineering shops.

Exposure or hypothermia results from prolonged cold conditions usually when the victim is wet. The sufferer may show signs of incoherence, uncharacteristic behavior, severe bouts of shivering, and lack of coordination as the body temperature in the core drops. Once on a mountain rescue I found one of a party stumbling along a ridge suffering from exposure. He had no idea where he was, swore and fought with me as I attempted to get him inside a sleeping bag in a shelter I erected, and could give no information about the others. After twenty minutes of warmth and hot sweet drinks, his behavior returned to normal. Immersion, with the wet clothes still on, in a bath just above normal body temperature, produces the most rapid recovery.

High-altitude sickness is an unpleasant and dangerous condition. At high altitude the air contains less oxygen and breathing becomes more difficult. The climber may feel weak, cough, suffer from vomiting and headache, and be unable to sleep. A slow ascent to a lower altitude often prevents discomfort. An excellent booklet by Larry Penberthy of Mountain Safety Research which is a reprint of the M.S.R. newsletter shows that many problems of altitude are related to an increased acidity of the body and can be combatted by the intake of an alkali such as Rolaids. A good fluid intake of three or four quarts a day, together with adequate food supplies, is essential. If preventative measures such as are

discussed in Penberthy's booklet lead to no improvement, then a rapid descent is the only safe course. High-altitude pulmonary edema, a condition in which the lungs fill with fluid can occur even at altitudes as low as 10,000 feet. Preliminary conditioning by exercise at altitude is the most important preventative.

In all mountain activities morale is a very important factor in survival. Remember that you are part of a team, be alert to the problems of your companions and be prepared to encourage and reassure them in the event of difficulties. A cheerful companion in a tight spot is worth more than almost any item of equipment. Hazards and ailments apart, the mountaineer has to consider many things that can be safely ignored by the climber on short technical rock or ice routes.

An expert knowledge of map reading and the ability to use a compass are essential skills. Many times, having set out in brilliant weather, I have been forced to make the descent after the climb in such poor visibility that, without a map and compass, success would have been impossible. A friend, who before a climb claimed to know the mountain like the back of his hand, had to suffer our relieved laughter after an all-night search when we discovered he had descended with great difficulty into the wrong valley. Acquire a good compass such as the Silva and learn how to use it accurately. Always carry a detailed map of the area you intend to climb in and a guidebook, if one is available, to the routes on the mountain. Many aspects of mountaineering cannot be dealt with adequately in a book. As your experience increases you will find that you are able to judge the time you need to complete a climb and the best route to follow.

There is no rule of thumb to give an estimate of the time necessary to climb a difficult route, but I usually find, on the ascent to the mountain, that if I allow for a pace of three miles an hour and add an hour for every thousand feet of ascent, I am not far wrong. On this basis, a climb with a pack to a high camp involving a distance of five miles and a rise of

4,500 feet would take six hours ten minutes to complete.

On the mountain itself, a preliminary study of photographs and route descriptions should provide a basis for the ascent. Often, it is hard to judge your position on the mountain. In some areas, such as Yosemite, a pitch-by-pitch description is available, but this is unusual. Usually, only general details are given, and you have to be alert for the best line. Keep a tally of the number of rope lengths you have run out; this will help you to estimate where you are. There is probably no substitute for speaking to someone who has climbed the route before you. You may, on the other hand, prefer the added thrill of making a route up a face or ridge of which you have no previous knowledge. Certainly, too detailed a route description can remove much of the challenge. For this reason many climbers try to climb where no one has gone before. After a time your eye will begin to pick out possible lines, and you will be able to estimate with a fair degree of accuracy whether they will be within your ability. An experienced companion willing to share his or her knowledge will be worth more than anything I can write on the decisions to be made in route finding.

Chapter 15

INTERLUDE: ROCKY MOUNTAIN NATIONAL PARK, COLORADO

From our high bivouac at 10,500 feet below the Andrews Glacier, about ten miles from Estes Park, Colorado, we could look up at our climb for the next day. In the cold of the October evening it rose stark and steep, the snow in its gullies and cracks catching the starlight.

The Sharkstooth. We had been looking at it for an hour, Will and I. When we arrived at our camp for the night, the last glow of the sun was bathing the top fifty feet of the 12,000-foot peak in a rosy light. The first major snowfall of the winter had clothed the surrounding slopes and filled the steep gully leading up to the peak, but the peak itself rose, black and forbidding above the white. Next morning, in the dark, we stumbled around on stiff limbs cooking a warm breakfast and packing items that we suddenly decided we would need. Soon, with our backpacks stowed behind a large rock, we kicked our way up the steepening slope to the col on the ridge to start the ascent. Several inches of new snow lay on old summer-hardened ice. Trying to make good time we did not rope up. The starts of climbs are often like this. Head down, with lungs gasping for air; ice axe freezing to wool mitt. Stomach complaining from exercise too soon after breakfast, or from anxiety about the hard day ahead. Little conversation. A blanking out of the mind.

We twisted our way upward, traversing over rock steps on unstable snow, floundering in deep cracks filled with powder. At last, on the col, we came alive. The morning sun behind us illuminated Longs Peak, and we felt its warmth seep into our bones. We had no guidebook with us, only a sketchy description of the route, and as we looked up at the steep rock walls above us the way to the summit was not obvious.

Eventually, after a snack and some debate, Will tied on to the rope and set off up a series of cracks and ledges leading across the north face. I had been more in favor of the southern ridge which was already bathed in sun, but action was what we needed, not discussion. He ran out the full length of the 150-foot rope and belayed securely on a good ledge.

When I arrived there, I stopped only to collect an assortment of slings and chocks and pressed on. On a high mountain, especially in October when snow clouds are scudding across the sky it's important to move fast. Anyway I was still cold, the more so since I had had to take off my mitts to grip on the small holds. As I climbed I warmed up and, for the first time that morning, began to enjoy myself. I continued the traverse heading for a crack and chimney system that split the face.

The rock was very good rough granite and its numerous holds enabled me for the most part to avoid the snow and ice. Looking up

(R. Shaw)

Sharkstooth above Estes Park, Colorado. A fine 12,000-foot rock peak with a coating of fall snow. (*R. Shaw*)

(S. Hilbert. Courtesy, Idaho State University Outdoor Program)

one could see little except rock; downward the scene was wintry with all the ledges banked high with fresh snow. Once in the crack, I found a good spike and belayed to that and to a large chock which I jammed securely behind a flake.

Up came Will, quickly and easily and climbed on, obviously less affected by the alti-tude than I was. Rope length after rope length we climbed toward the ridge with our situa-tion becoming more airy. As the face steep-ened there was less evidence of snow. A shout from Will that he had discovered a piton told us that we were on the correct route. Delicate slabs topped steep walls; deep ice choked chimneys slanted toward the gray

(*S. Hilbert. Courtesy, Idaho State University Outdoor Program*)

sky. A few flakes of snow fell, spurring us on. Would we make it to the top before a real blizzard started?

Some pitches later the crack we were following ended in a large overhang. Will belayed below it, and as I climbed toward him, I became nervous about the prospect of leading the next pitch. The sack with the food and the emergency clothing seemed to grow heavier on my back. Well, we could always retreat. I had carefully noted the position of anchors we could use to rappel off if it proved necessary to descend the face. Still it would be disappointing not to complete the climb.

When I reached him, Will was on a minute ledge fixed to an assortment of belays. There was no place for me to stand while we changed over the sack. To the left of the crack a steep slab seemed to offer some possibility of avoiding the overhang, so I stepped delicately onto some small holds on its edge, awed by the thousand-foot drop below my feet. Gingerly, I moved up and across the slab. Better holds appeared leading around a corner. I hesitated. The wind tugged at the hood of my parka.

"How does it look?" Will shouted from behind me.

"Oh, it'll go." I heard myself say and began to balance delicately up the rounded holds. Two or three moves and I had my left hand securely on a good ledge. I was up. Above me a crack with large holds led toward the ridge. The sun broke through the clouds as Will joined me on a broad platform.

Several rope lengths later Will threaded his way through an intricate pitch of overhangs and dihedrals and we arrived at the ridge. It was a knife edge falling away steeply on both sides. We perched on the ridge eating some candy and looking down to the little patch of green where we had pitched the tent the night before. A raven swept past, its feathers fluttering as it dived on the wind. The rest of the ridge was easier and we unroped to gain better speed.

Clouds skimmed the summit; it was no place to linger. With snow flakes whirling around us we began to search for the best way down. We had been told that there were rappel bolts just below the summit, and after a short search we found them. At this point we began to regret bringing only one rope. With it doubled we could only descend seventy-five feet at a time.

Will launched himself off first, disappearing over the lip. I looked at the bolts anxiously, and tried to crane over the edge to see how he was faring. After a time I heard him call that he was off the rope and I started down.

Rappelling is one of the more dangerous mountain activities. It is essential that the anchor is checked thoroughly and that on the descent as little strain as possible is put on it. When I reached Will, he had already fixed another anchor and I set off down.

Rappel followed rappel. Frequently, because of the inadequate length of our rope, we had to climb down to find another anchor. Once we had to swing sideways from the end of the rope to get to a ledge. More seriously, several times we had to rely on shaky anchors.

At last we arrived on the col. To relax in a safe position after hours of tenseness and concentration is one of the great mountain pleasures. We sat in the snow munching nuts and chocolate and quenching our thirst. Inside, we had that swelling bubble of joy that comes from having, in good company, found the way to the summit of a difficult mountain and descended safely. Hours before we had sat on this same narrow pass, full of doubts and uncertainties, cold and apprehensive.

Now, as we picked up our ice axes and began the descent to our camp, the remembrance of tiredness and clumsy movements, of fear and cold faded, and we were left with memories of shapely rock, or sure holds, of catlike movements on steep slabs, of airy corners and exhilarating drops, and, most of all, of experiences shared.

Appendix 1

CLIMBING SCHOOLS

For the beginning climber probably the best action is to enroll for a course at a climbing school or to join a climbing club that provides instruction for its members. An experienced climber, especially one used to teaching the sport, can see and correct faults in technique that act as a brake on ability. A course at a school will not turn the novice into a brilliant and safe mountaineer; but it may lay the foundations. Moreover, what the novice needs most of all to sustain and encourage his mountaineering, is the company of like-minded people who can suggest routes, mount expeditions, and provide the breadth of knowledge that goes to make up a competent mountaineer.

ALPINE CRAFTS LTD., P.O. Box 85697, North Vancouver, British Columbia, Canada.

APPALACHIAN CLIMBING SCHOOL, Mountaineering South, Inc., 344 Tunnel Road, Asheville, NC 28805.

BASE CAMP CLIMBING SCHOOL, 121 North Mole Street, Philadelphia, PA 19102.

BOB CULP CLIMBING SCHOOL, 1329 Broadway, Boulder, CO 80302.

CANADIAN SCHOOL OF MOUNTAINEERING LTD., P.O. Box 1552, Banff, Alberta, Canada.

CLIMB HIGH, INC., MOUNTAINEERING SCHOOL, 277 Main Street, Burlington, VT 05401.

COLORADO MOUNTAIN SCHOOL, 2402 Dotsero Avenue, Loveland, CO 80537.

EASTERN MOUNTAIN SPORTS CLIMBING SCHOOL, INC., Main Street, North Conway, NH 03860.

EXUM MOUNTAIN GUIDE SERVICE AND SCHOOL OF AMERICAN MOUNTAINEERING, Moose, WY 83012.

FANTASY RIDGE SCHOOL OF ALPINISM, P.O. Box 2104, Estes Park, CO 80517.

FORWARD SCHOOL OF MOUNTAINEERING, 1432 Tweed Street, Colorado Springs, CO 80909.

HARVEY T. CARTER CLIMBING SCHOOL, P.O. Box 962, Aspen, CO 81611.

INSTITUTE OF MOUNTAIN EDUCATION, P.O. Box 336, Eldorado Springs, CO 80025.

INTERNATIONAL MOUNTAIN EQUIPMENT, INC., P.O. Box 494, Main Street, North Conway, NH 03860.

JACKSON HOLE MOUNTAIN GUIDES, Teton Village, WY 83025.

LUTE JERSTAD ADVENTURES, INC., P.O. Box 19527, Portland, OR 97219.

MOUNT ADAMS WILDERNESS INSTITUTE, INC., Flying L. Ranch, Glenwood, WA 98619.

MOUNTAIN AFFAIR MOUNTAINEERING SCHOOL, 54414 North Circle Drive, P.O. Box 369, Idyllwild, CA 92349.

MOUNTAIN CRAFT, P.O. Box 622, Davis, CA 95616.

MOUNTAIN SCHOOL, P.O. Box 728, Renton, WA 98005.

Instructor and student nearing the top of the Potato Masher. Upper Yosemite Falls is in the background. (*Courtesy, Yosemite Park and Curry Company*)

MOUNT WHITNEY GUIDE SERVICE AND SIERRA NEVADA SCHOOL OF MOUNTAINEERING, P.O. Box 659, Lone Pine, CA 93545.

NATIONAL OUTDOOR LEADERSHIP SCHOOL, P.O. Box AA, Lander, WY 82520.

NORD ALP, INC., 3260 Main Street, Buffalo, NY 14214.

NORTH COUNTRY MOUNTAINEERING, INC., P.O. Box 951, Hanover, NH 03755.

OUTWARD BOUND, INC., National Headquarters, 165 West Putnam Avenue, Greenwich, CT 06830.

PALISADE SCHOOL OF MOUNTAINEERING, 1398 Solano Avenue, Albany, CA 94706.

POTOMAC VALLEY CLIMBING SCHOOL, INC., P.O. Box 5622, Washington, DC 20016.

RAINIER MOUNTAINEERING, INC., 201 St. Helens, Tacoma, WA 98402.

ROCKCRAFT, 609 Durant Street, Modesto, CA 95350.

RUDI GERTSCH MOUNTAINEERING SCHOOL, P.O. Box 543, Banff, Alberta, Canada.

SAWTOOTH MOUNTAINEERING, INC., 5200 Fairview Avenue Mini Mall, Boise, ID 83704.

TOO DISTANT HORIZON CLIMBING SCHOOL, 3401 Valley View Drive, Morietia, GA 33006.

YOSEMITE MOUNTAINEERING, Yosemite, CA 95389.

Appendix 2

MOUNTAINEERING CLUBS

The following list includes most of the well-established clubs in North America. Many of them are happy to welcome beginning climbers; others demand experience and skill. There are countless other clubs, and the local equipment store should be able to advise you of these. In addition, many universities and colleges have mountaineering clubs and occasionally Outdoor Programs that run courses for non-students. Notable among these last are the University of Oregon, Eugene, and Idaho State University, Pocatello.

ADIRONDACK MOUNTAIN CLUB, INC., 172 Ridge Street, Glens Falls, NY 12801.

ALPINE CLUB OF CANADA, P.O. Box 1026, Banff, Alberta, Canada.

AMERICAN ALPINE CLUB, 113 East 90th Street, New York, NY 10028.

APPALACHIAN MOUNTAIN CLUB, 5 Joy Street, Boston, MA 02108.

ARIZONA MOUNTAINEERING CLUB, 4225 South Forty-seventh Place, Phoenix, AZ 85040.

CHICAGO MOUNTAINEERING CLUB, 2801 South Parkway, Chicago, IL 60616.

CLEVELAND MOUNTAINEERS, c/o Adlers Camping Inc., 728 Prospect Avenue, Cleveland, OH 44115.

COLORADO MOUNTAIN CLUB, 1723 East 16th Avenue, Denver, CO 80218.

EXPLORERS CLUB OF PITTSBURGH, c/o Mountain Trail Shop, 5435 Walnut Street, Pittsburgh, PA 15232.

GREEN MOUNTAIN CLUB, 108 Merchants Row, Rutland, VT 05701.

IDAHO ALPINE CLUB, Idaho Falls, ID 83401.

IOWA MOUNTAINEERS, P.O. Box 163, Iowa City, IA 52240.

MAZAMAS, 909 North West 19th Street, Portland; OR 97207.

MOUNTAINEERING CLUB OF ALASKA, P.O. Box 2037, Anchorage, AK 99510.

MOUNTAIN CLUB OF MARYLAND, c/o H.H. Camper Haven, 424 North Eutaw Street, Baltimore, MD 21201.

MOUNTAINEERS, 719 Pike Street, Seattle, WA 98101.

NEW MEXICO MOUNTAIN CLUB, P.O. Box 4151, Albuquerque, NM 87112.

NORTHSTAR MOUNTAINEERS, c/o Midwest Mountaineering, 1408 Hennepin Avenue, Minneapolis, MN 55403.

OBSIDIANS, Lane YMCA, Eugene, OR 97403.

SIERRA CLUB, 1050 Mills Tower, 220 Bush Street, San Francisco, CA 94101.

WASATCH MOUNTAIN CLUB, c/o Dr. Paul Horton, 3155 Highland Drive, Salt Lake City, UT 84106.

(S. Hilbert. Courtesy, Idaho State University Outdoor Program)

Appendix 3

RECOMMENDED CLIMBING AREAS

The following is a list of the more popular climbing areas in the United States. It omits many worthwhile cliffs and mountains. In many mountainous and rocky areas the possibilities are almost endless. In Canada only the main areas have been mentioned as there is a profusion of rocks and mountains that can be climbed. For detailed information about the area you live in, the best approach is to contact your local equipment store.

ALABAMA

Great Smoky Mountains

ALASKA

Mount McKinley and many other large mountains
Porter Rock near Anchorage

ARIZONA

Camelback Mountain near Phoenix
Pinnacle Peak near Tempe
Granite Mountain near Prescott

CALIFORNIA

Many good climbing areas of which the most important are:
Yosemite
The High Sierra
Mission Gorge near Idyllwild
Joshua Tree National Monument
Santa Clara Valley
Tahquitz and Suicide Rocks
Pinnacles, Santa Cruz Mountains
Lovers' Leap, Strawberry

COLORADO

Many fine mountains and canyons
Boulder Canyon
Eldorado Springs Canyon, near Boulder
Rocky Mountain National Park, Estes
Black Canyon, near Montrose

CONNECTICUT

Lime Rock near Lakeville
Ragged Mountain near Southington

DISTRICT OF COLUMBIA

Carderock, Carderock State Park

GEORGIA

Tallulah Gorge, near Decatur
Mount Yunah, near Cleveland

IDAHO

Table Rock, near Boise
City of Rock, near Pocatello
The Sawtooths, near Stanley

ILLINOIS

Mississippi Palisades, in Savanna

INDIANA

Portland Arch, near Covington

KANSAS

Rock Quarries, near Topeka

MAINE

Bucks Ledge, near Locke Mills
Mount Katahdin, near Millinocket

Mount Kineo, near Moosehead Lake
Tumbledown Mountain, near Weld

MASSACHUSETTS

Black Rock, near Sheffield
Crow Hill, near Leominster
Barn Ledge, near Leverett
Quincy Quarries, in Quincy

MICHIGAN

Grand Ledge, near East Lansing

MINNESOTA

Taylor's Falls, near Minneapolis

MONTANA

The Mission Range
The Beartooths

NEBRASKA

Chimney Rock
Scotts Bluff National Monument

NEW HAMPSHIRE

White Horse Ledges, near North Conway
Cathedral Ledges, near North Conway
Cannon Cliff, near Franconia
Holt's Ledge, near Lyme

NEW JERSEY

Cranberry Ledge, near Flemington
Watershed, near Newfoundland

NEW MEXICO

Sandia Mountains, near Albuquerque
The Tooth of Time, Cimarron
The Basalts, near Santa Fé

NEW YORK

Chapel Pond, Adirondacks
Shawangunks, near New Palz
Bronx River, Botanical Gardens, Bronx
The Boulders, Central Park, Manhattan

NORTH CAROLINA

Linville Gorge, near Asheville
Table Rock, near Morgantown
Stone Mountain, near North Wilkesboro
Devil's Courthouse, near Brevard

OHIO

Clifton Gorge, John Brian State Park

OKLAHOMA

Chandler Park, Tulsa

OREGON

Three Finger Jack, near Bend
Obsidian Cliffs, near Bend
Smith Rocks, near Terrehome
Three Sisters Peaks, Mount Jefferson
Mount Hood, Portland

PENNSYLVANIA

Ralph Stover State Park, Upper Bucks County
Coburn Rock, near Pittsburgh

SOUTH DAKOTA

The Needles, Black Hills

TENNESSEE

Bee Rock, Monterey

TEXAS

Enchanted Rock, Fredericksburg

UTAH

Little Cottonwood Canyon, near Salt Lake City
Salt Lake Crags, near Salt Lake City
Wasatch Mountains

VERMONT

Bolton Rock, near Burlington
Smugglers' Notch, near Stowe
Willoughby Lake, near West Burke

WASHINGTON

Index Wall, near Seattle
Leavenworth
Granite Point, near Pullman
Minnehaha Rocks, near Spokane
The North Cascades
Mount Rainier

WEST VIRGINIA

Cooper Rocks, near Morgantown
Champe Rocks, near Seneca
Seneca Rock
Nelson Rocks, near Seneca

WISCONSIN

Gibraltar Rock, near Lodi
Baraboo Bluffs, near Madison
Devil's Lake State Park, near Madison

WYOMING

The Tetons
The Wind River Mountains
The Snowy Mountains

CANADA

Many fine mountain ranges from Baffin Island in the east to the British Columbian coastal ranges in the west:

The Bugaboos
The Rocky Mountains, Calgary
Squamish Chief, Vancouver
Mont Césaire, Quebec
Mont Condor, Quebec

Appendix 4

GUIDEBOOKS

In addition to those listed below, many smaller guidebooks, which give information on local outcrops, are in print. These can usually be purchased through the climbing store in the locality.

ALASKA

Mountaineering Club of Alaska, *55 Ways to the Wilderness in South Central Alaska* (Seattle: The Mountaineers).

CALIFORNIA

STEVE ROPER, *Climber's Guide to Yosemite Valley* (San Francisco: Sierra Club).

ALLEN STECK, *Guide to Mount Shasta* (San Francisco: Sierra Club).

HERVEY VOGE and ANDREW J. SMATKO, *Mountaineer's Guide to the High Sierra* (San Francisco: Sierra Club).

CHARLES WILTS, *Climber's Guide to Tahquitz and Suicide Rocks* (New York: American Alpine Club).

Climber's Guide to Joshua Tree (San Jacinto, CA, Arrow Printing Company).

Guide to Pinnacles (San Francisco: Sierra Club).

COLORADO

PAT AMENT and CLEVELAND MCCARTY, *High over Boulder* (Boulder: Pruett Press).

WALTER W. FRICKE, JR., *Climber's Guide to the Rocky Mountain National Park Area* (Boulder: Paddock).

ROBERT ORMES, *Guide to the Colorado Mountains* (Chicago: The Swallow Press).

NEW HAMPSHIRE

JOSEPH and KAREN COTE, *A Climber's Guide to Mount Washington Valley* (Topsfield, MA: Fox Run Press).

NEW YORK

TRUDY HEALY, *A Climber's Guide to the Adirondacks* (Glens Falls, Adirondack Mountain Club).

RICHARD C. WILLIAMS, *Climber's Guide to the Shawangunks* (New York: American Alpine Club).

PENNSYLVANIA

IVAN JIRAK, *Pittsburgh Area Climber's Guide* (Pittsburgh).

DAKOTA

BOB CAMPS, *Climber's Guide to the Needles in the Black Hills of Dakota* (New York: American Alpine Club).

UTAH

DAVID R. SMITH, *Climber's Guide to the Salt Lake Granite* (Salt Lake City: Wasatch Publishers).

WASHINGTON

FRED BECKEY, *Cascade Alpine Guide* (Seattle: The Mountaineers).

TOM MILLER, *The North Cascades* (Seattle: The Mountaineers).

WYOMING

LEE ORTENBERGER, *Climber's Guide to the Tetons* (San Francisco: Sierra Club).

CANADA

D. CULBERT, *Climber's Guide to Coastal Ranges of British Columbia* (Banff, Alberta: Alpine Club of Canada).

W. PUTNAM, *Climber's Guide to Rocky Mountains of Canada—North* (New York: American Alpine Club).

————, *Climber's Guide to Rocky Mountains of Canada—South* (New York: American Alpine Club).

Climber's Guide to Interior Ranges of British Columbia—North (New York: American Alpine Club).

Climber's Guide to Interior Ranges of British Columbia—South (New York: American Alpine Club).

The city of Rock, Alma, Idaho. A paradise of rock for all abilities. (*R. Shaw*)

Smith Rocks, Oregon. (*Courtesy, Lute Jerstad Adventures*)

Appendix 5

SUPPLIERS OF MOUNTAINEERING EQUIPMENT

Most communities of any size in North America now have an outdoor-sports store that retails mountaineering equipment. This list is very selective and includes the main suppliers who carry on a mail-order business in addition to retailing through stores. Some of those listed, such as Forrest Mountaineering and Great Pacific Iron Works, are manufacturers of quality mountaineering equipment as well as retailers of other lines.

EDDIE BAUER EXPEDITION OUTFITTER, 1926 Third Street, Seattle, WA 98101.

BECK OUTDOOR PRODUCTS, P.O. Box 1038, Crescent City, CA 95530.

BISHOPS ULTIMATE OUTDOOR EQUIPMENT, Box 4, Oakton, VA 22124.

BLACKS, 225 Strathcona Avenue, Ottawa 1, Ontario, Canada.

CAMP 7, INC., 3235 Prairie Avenue, Boulder, CO 80302.

CAMP TRAILS, P.O. Box 14500, Phoenix, AZ 85063.

CHUCK ROAST EQUIPMENT, P.O. Box 224, North Conway, NH 03818.

CLASS 5 MOUNTAINEERING EQUIPMENT, 2010 Seventh Street, Berkeley, CA 94710.

COLORADO MOUNTAIN INDUSTRIES (CMI), 1896 Reading Road, Cincinatti, OH 45215.

EASTERN MOUNTAIN SPORTS, Vose Farm Road, Peterborough, NH 03458.

FORREST MOUNTAINEERING, LTD., 1517 Platte Street, Denver, CO 80202.

GREAT PACIFIC IRON WORKS, Chouinard Equipment for Alpinists, P.O. Box 150, Ventura, CA 93001.

HOLUBAR MOUNTAINEERING, LTD., 1875 Thirtieth Street, Boulder, CO 80302.

INTERNATIONAL MOUNTAIN EQUIPMENT, INC., P.O. Box 494, Main Street, North Conway, NH 03860.

KALMAR TRADING CORPORATION, P.O. Box 77343, Department CSB, San Francisco, CA 94107.

KELTY MOUNTAINEERING, 1801 Victory Boulevard, Glendale, CA 91201.

LEEPER EQUIPMENT, Wall Street, Boulder, CO 80302.

LOWE ALPINE SYSTEMS, 1752 N. Fifty-fifth Street, Boulder, CO 80301.

MOUNTAIN PARAPHERNALIA, 906 Durant Street, Modesto, CA 95352.

MOUNTAIN SAFETY RESEARCH, INC., 631 South Ninety-sixth Street, Seattle, WA 98108.

NORTH FACE, 1234 Fifth Street, Berkeley, CA 94710.

RECREATIONAL EQUIPMENT, INC., CO-OP, 1525 Eleventh Avenue, Seattle, WA 98122.

(R. Shaw)

SEATTLE MANUFACTURING CORPORATION, 12880 Northrup Way, Bellevue, WA 98005.

SIERRA DESIGNS, Fourth and Addison, Berkeley, CA 94710.

STEPHENSON'S WARMLITE, RFD 4, P.O. Box 398, Winnipesqukee Highlands, Gilford, NH 03246.

TRAILWISE—THE SKI HUT, 1615 University Avenue, Berkeley, CA 94703.

Appendix 6

RECOMMENDED READING

BOB GODFREY and DUDLEY CHELTON, *Climb* (Boulder, CO: Alpine House, 1978).

R. L. G. IRVING, *The Romance of Mountaineering* (New York: E. P. Dutton & Co., Inc., 1935).

CHRIS JONES, *Climbing in North America* (Berkeley, CA: University of California Press, 1976).

HARVEY MANNING, ed., *The Freedom of the Hills* (Seattle: The Mountaineers, 1975).

WILFRID NOYCE and IAN MCMORRIN, *World Atlas of Mountaineering* (London: Thomas Nelson, 1969).

GASTON REBUFFAT, *On Snow and Rock* (New York: Oxford University Press, 1963).

ROYAL ROBBINS, *Advanced Rockcraft* (Glendale, CA: La Siesta Press, 1973).

DAVE ROBERTS, *The Mountain of My Fear* (New York: Vanguard Press, 1968).

GALEN ROWELL, ed., *The Vertical World of Yosemite: A Collection of Photographs and Writings on Rock Climbing in Yosemite* (Berkeley, CA: Wilderness Press, 1974).

ANNE SCHNEIDER and STEVEN SCHNEIDER, *The Climber's Sourcebook* (New York: Doubleday & Company, Inc., 1976).

HOWARD SNYDER, *The Hall of the Mountain King* (New York: Charles Scribner's Sons, 1973).

JAMES RAMSEY ULLMAN, *Straight Up. John Harlin: The Life and Death of a Mountaineer* (New York: Doubleday & Company, Inc., 1968).

MIRIAM UNDERHILL, *Give Me the Hills* (London: Methuen, 1956).

JAMES A. WILKERSON, M.D., ed., *Medicine for Mountaineering* (Seattle: The Mountaineers, 1967).

WALTER A. WOOD, *A History of Mountaineering in the Saint Elias Mountains* (Banff, Alberta: Alpine Club of Canada).

PERIODICALS

The American Alpine Journal (American Alpine Club, New York).

Ascent (Sierra Club, San Francisco).

Canadian Alpine Journal (Alpine Club of Canada, Banff, Alberta, Canada).

Mountain (56 Sylvester Road, London, N2, England).

Off Belay (12416 169th Avenue SE, Renton, WA 98055).

Summit (Box 1889, Big Bear Lake, CA 92315).

BOOKLETS

Bradford Washburn, *Frostbite: What It Is—How to Prevent It—Emergency Treatment* (Boston: The Museum of Science).

Larry Penberthy, *Mountain Safety Research Newsletter* (Seattle: M.S.R. 631 South 96th Street, Seattle, WA 98108).

Cathedral Peak, the Sierras. (*R. Shaw*)